Centred

Centred

*How to **Lead** with **Confidence** in times of **Complex Change***

SUSANNE LE BOUTILLIER

First published 2024

Cover design by Sylvie Veit

Typesetting by BookPOD

ISBN: 978-1-7637750-0-8 (paperback) eISBN: 978-1-7637750-1-5(e-book)

A catalogue record for this book is available from the National Library of Australia

CONTENTS

INTRODUCTION

From storm tossed to centred calm – finding your strength in the eye of the storm

Remember the George Clooney movie where he captained the Andrea Gail, a fishing vessel that disappeared?

The movie was based on a true story where Captain Frank W. 'Billy' Tyne decided to stick to his plan in the face of weather that looked wicked. Billy knew several weather systems were all heading for his location – Hurricane Grace over Bermuda, a cold front and a storm over the Great Lakes. It looked pretty touch and go, but he had 40,000 pounds of fish on board and a malfunctioning ice machine.

He had a choice to make, and he decided to save his catch.

However, the different weather systems evolved as they interacted. Their direction and nature changed multiple times, eventually emerging as a superstorm known as the Halloween Storm or the 1991 Perfect Storm.

Although timely warnings from the National Weather Service saved countless lives during that perfect storm, Captain Billy Tyne's decision to continue on proved fatal for him and his crew.[1]

Like Billy Tyne, many leaders facing their own 'perfect storm' wonder whether they'll make the right decisions and how those decisions will affect them, their team, their organisation and their lives outside of work. They wonder whether they have the skills to stop them from going down with the ship.

---

1   Houghton, G. (2003). *Wreck of the Andrea Gail: Three Days of a Perfect Storm.* Rosen Publishing Group.

Navigating work and life today can feel like captaining a ship lost in a storm – one where many familiar landmarks have vanished or are quickly disappearing. But with every storm – even the perfect storm – there is an eye.

In the eye of the storm, where chaos swirls and challenges loom on every side, lies a place of calm and clarity – a place where you – as a leader – can centre yourself, find your true strength and determine your next right step. This is the goal, the continuous destination, of centred leadership.

The world is complex. Leading change and personal growth are also complex and *will* see you in the storm. And while you can't avoid the storm, when you know yourself, you can recentre in the calm of the eye and carry on despite the storm.

Unfortunately, I didn't always know that myself. Instead, I spent years being buffeted by winds, rain, hail and unexpected flying objects, until I ultimately succumbed. Until I lost my ability to perform at my best. I burnt out. I was lost in the storm. But what I learned changed the course of my life and my career.

How did I end up lost in the storm?

2019

It's mid-2019. I'm sitting in a conference room full of colleagues with smiling faces, chatting to each other. But I sit there, tears steadily tracking down my cheeks and into my collarbone.

We were in the middle of driving multiple complex projects. As a senior executive, I had people relying on me to keep everything moving and get results. I didn't have time to burn out. I didn't have time for whatever this was.

Yet here I was, lost in the storm. How did this happen?

Thirty years before

After finishing university, I had planned on becoming a high school drama teacher, but I didn't get through the auditions. I decided I could live without it when the boy who played my husband in our high school musical ended his life when he also failed to get through.

Instead, I fell into working in the health industry while treading water and working out what I really wanted to pursue. But the health industry proved to be fertile ground. The opportunities were abundant. I found that it was a good place to use my energy and drive. And I found that I was good at the work. I threw myself with enthusiasm into every challenging assignment thrown my way.

Fifteen years before

My rise to middle management was relatively quick. I have been lucky, but I also love to learn. I work hard and I dedicate myself to the task at hand. Because of this, senior leaders continued to see my potential and give me opportunities. It wasn't long before a combination of hard work and making the most of those opportunities saw me rise to the senior executive ranks. I was on my way, doing a job I was good at and helping to drive change and make a difference.

From star performer to burning star

Over the years, as I continued to grow in my career, people would casually comment that I was a star performer. Of course, I didn't believe them – it felt like false flattery. It was just hard work and good luck, wasn't it?

The result of the attention meant that from my perspective I had far more to lose if I failed. I had to keep achieving to feel I was doing enough. But more importantly, to feel that *I was enough*.

Driven by purpose and wanting to make a positive difference, I passionately believed I could help change the system from the inside. Combined together, this passion and drive led me to push myself harder and harder, working more and more hours and striving to accomplish everything that I felt the organisation and my team needed.

My time as the interim chief executive of a new entity requiring me to create quality clinical training capacity for the health system was one of my favourite roles. The more I did, the more work was thrown my way. And the more work that was thrown my way, the more I pushed myself to take it on and accomplish it well. I spent vast amounts of time filling emergent gaps, managing risks and ensuring deliverables were just right. When I took a moment to catch my breath, sometimes at 8 or 9pm at night, I found that there was almost no breath to take. In the years to come I discovered that these were the early nights.

I felt the rug was pulled out from under me when I was told I was being given a different role. One which later proved to be an amazing development opportunity. However, at the time I was devastated and sought support from an executive coach. I remember telling them that I was worried about not being as stimulated in the new role. I should have been more careful about what I wished for.

The roller coaster ride continued.

I was exhausted. There were moments of happiness, but I was not happy. I was torn in so many different directions – kids, partner, team, family, friends and, almost above all at times, keeping all those people above me in the organisation happy.

Soon the busyness became my normal. It's what I knew and even where I began to be comfortable because the busyness defined me, it defined my worthiness as a person. And of course, I couldn't let anyone down. Yet I longed for time and space to be myself and the leader I wanted to be instead of trying to keep everyone happy.

Things likely came to a head, when after over twenty-five years, it was time to get uncomfortable in a less familiar agency. I made the move from a lead role in one of the largest health organisations in the country to a social services organisation impacted by significant national policy change and constantly described in the media as in crisis.

The change started well and for a couple of years it was okay. But moving to a senior executive role in this new organisation brought me even closer to people experiencing vulnerability in the midst of a hugely complex situation. The organisation was going through massive upheaval trying to achieve transformational and systemic change. And I was thrust into the middle of the chaos. This was nothing new but that move amplified my reactive tendencies.

I found myself working even harder and longer and finding that it took more and more to make me feel like I was achieving my personal goals and those of my team and organisation. Whilst being expected to deliver multiple transformational changes, the number of people available to do the work kept reducing and the workload kept increasing. Stakeholder expectations about delivery timeframes were unreasonable and stayed that way, and while the media reported crisis after crisis, the powers above had high expectations they would be fixed – quickly and easily.

The creeping clouds

Unbeknownst to me, the shadow of my reactive tendencies was spreading, like storm clouds moving in. The intensity of the situation meant I was stuck in a cycle of trying to respond, but fire after fire meant that I was often pushing myself to my limit (and beyond). I began to lose my objectivity and instead of considering the right action and next steps to take, I would sometimes respond unconsciously – reacting instead of acting. And the consistency in my decision making decreased as the speed of the cycles increased their momentum.

I was stuck in the cycle and the cycle was beyond what could be successfully managed. My reactive tendencies and the shadow I cast around me had helped me lead in a complex environment up to a point. However, the sun had literally shifted, and I was casting a much longer and broader shadow than usual. And I was somewhat oblivious because I was so focused on delivering and surviving.

After eighteen months, something had to give. And so that's how I found myself sitting in a boardroom with tears running down my face in 2019.

What was really going on

A colleague asked me what was going on. They could see the tears rolling down my cheeks.

I told them, 'I don't know why my eyes are leaking – it's been happening on and off'.

And I truly didn't know why the tears were rolling down my face. I felt fine (we all know what that means!).

When I eventually asked my doctor, she told me my body was reacting to sustained and chronic stress. She even used the words post-traumatic. I wouldn't stop, so my body decided to tell me enough was enough.

I was burned out, and the only way to recover was to stop.

I had to let go and rest if I wanted to recover.

But, of course, I didn't stop.

Instead of listening to my doctor, I told my boss I would wait two weeks to take leave so I could do enough to hand everything over to the person backfilling me. I couldn't just leave the work to someone else. It seemed inconceivable to me that I could simply walk away and take the time I needed to become well again. I was still completely caught up in reacting to the context.

I learned the hard way that systems are complex, and ambiguity and uncertainty are rife in every organisation. As a leader, not everything you try works, and you have to learn to be agile with change, to roll with the punches and not take it personally when things don't go your way.

But more importantly even than all of this is learning to centre yourself despite the storms raging around you. To learn that the situation is not _you;_ that you are not your context. I had known this for years, but I succumbed to the busyness and forgot.

The good news is you are not your context

This book is designed to help leaders understand that you are not your context. You are not the situation that you find yourself in.

When you face your own challenging context, and you will, can you find a way to pull back? Do you have people who act as an early warning system who let you know when you need to reset and respond? Or are all the people around you focused on their own survival?

If you are finding yourself buckling under the storms that are besetting all leaders today, understand you are not alone. Stories like this are sadly becoming more common across all types of organisations. All around the globe, leaders, from start-ups to established corporations to government agencies, are grappling with a landscape in flux. It doesn't matter whether you're in a large corporation, a public sector agency, a not-for-profit organisation or a small to medium business.

Leaders are falling into the trap of being shaped by the context whirling around them every day. And many of them are finding themselves lost in the storm, just as I was.

But the good news is you have a choice. And when you understand these two things, first, that you are not your context, and second, that you have a choice, then you are in a position to take steps to find your own centre – to become what I will refer to throughout the book as a 'centred leader'. And as a centred leader you'll be able to find the eye, even while the storm continues to rage around you.

It is never too late to learn to connect or reconnect with yourself, notice how you're reacting and make a different choice about how you want to be experienced by others. It starts with self-awareness, self-reflection, staying tethered to your values and being guided by the Centring Star so you can make sense of your context, consciously connect and stay open to revelations. You know – those 'aha' moments that give you confidence you're taking the next right step.

This book will help you to see that it's possible to master integrating the person you want to be with how others experience you while you lead yourself through the volatility, complexity, ambiguity and uncertainty of work and life.

And when you do this, you will no longer feel like you're at the centre of a perfect storm or wonder how you keep finding yourself in this position. You won't have to dig as deep to gather the energy to find your way through yet another emerging storm. You'll have the tools and techniques to centre yourself and feel safe to venture out from the eye of the storm, again and again.

Though my experience with burnout has been the catalyst for my research into centred leadership and my drive to share how we can do better, it wasn't my only experience with challenging and complex work contexts. Over the years, I have often felt like I'm in a perfect storm. And as a leader today, so will you.

My hope is that this book will be your guide to show you why you need to centre yourself in the ever-changing landscape our world presents to us and how to navigate between the eyes of multiple merging storms successfully to become a centred leader.

I will introduce you to the Centring Star framework which has been designed to enable you to find that calm space amidst the chaos, move intentionally and strategically through the storm to the next eye, and stay tethered to what makes you uniquely you – your values and character strengths.

Let's get started.

PART 1
THE STORM

CHAPTER 1

Context is Everything

In his play *Man and Superman*, George Bernard Shaw said:

> *'The only man who behaves sensibly is my tailor, he takes my measurements anew every time he sees me. The rest go on with their old measurements and expected them to fit me'.*[2]

No one likes it when others label them, but particularly when they're labelling them based on what they've seen in a single specific situation.

So, when it comes to centring ourselves and our leadership, we need to recognise first and foremost that no one is wholly the person they appear to be in a specific context, including – and especially – you.

Context matters, but it doesn't need to define us... unless we let it.

But the challenge is that we're also in a world of rapid change. We're in a storm.

---

2   Shaw, G. (1903). *Man and Superman*. Archibald Constable & Co.

Decade of turbulence and decreasing trust

COVID-19 may have moved from pandemic to endemic. However, that doesn't mean the world will return to how it was before. It has never been static, and today we're seeing continual changes at an exponential level. In fact, the pace of change we're experiencing now is faster than ever before.[3] Of course, whether this will lead to continued improvements in the human condition remains to be seen.

Various reports from the World Economic Forum, Bain and Co, McKinsey and Gartner all paint the next decade as a complex tapestry of challenge and change. At a global level, we are seeing or expect to see the re-emergence of dormant threats, including:

- Inflation and increases in the cost of living.

- Geopolitical confrontation on a scale not seen for decades.

- An increase in the intensity of social unrest. In the last five years, we've already seen mass protests across the globe in response to racially motivated police brutality and institutionalised racism and in support of women's rights, climate action and public health.

- The spectre of nuclear warfare.[4]

---

3 Roser, M. (27 February 2023). 'Emerging Technologies: This timeline charts the fast pace of tech transformation across centuries.' World Economic Forum. https://www.weforum.org/agenda/2023/02/this-timeline-charts-the-fast-pace-of-tech-transformation-across-centuries/.

4 (10 January 2024). 'Global Risks Report 2024.' [Report]. World Economic Forum. https://www.weforum.org/publications/global-risks-report-2024/; (2024). '2Q24 Emerging Risks Report.' [Report]. Gartner. https://www.gartner.com/en/audit-risk/trends/top-emerging-risk-trends-for-erm-leaders.

Yet, few of this generation's business leaders and policy makers are experienced in responding to these risks. The terrain is unfamiliar, and what worked before is unlikely to work in the same way again.

Layered over these risks there are new challenges to contend with, including:

- High debt levels straining government budgets that could lead to reduced public services, increased taxes or borrowing to repay debt.

- Slowing economic growth.

- For the first time ever the United Nations Development Program reporting a decline in the global Human Development Index (HDI) value for two consecutive years.

- A shift in the geographic availability of future talent pools. The World Economic Forum predicts that by 2040, much of the working-age population will be in Africa, South America and Asia. However, regions like Europe, the United Kingdom, the United States and Australia that rely on migrant talent today do not have strong connections to the countries that will become their future talent hubs.

- Rapid and unconstrained development of technology, such as generative artificial intelligence (AI), and the risks associated with concentrations of cloud-based services with limited numbers of vendors in limited locations. Associated risks range from unintended consequences of training generative AI, like embedding pre-existing prejudice and bias, service failure and the negative effects of government intervention or lack of action.

- Rapid and dramatic shifts in the skills needed by the workforce of the future and the inability to meet demand due to constraints related to time and investment.

- Consumer-driven expectations about social and environmental issues like climate change and climate ambitions leading to the expansion of environmental, social and governance standards.[5]

As leaders all this matters.

It's the context in which we're trying to do our work, lead our teams and create great outcomes for our organisations and even for ourselves. But each of these challenges layers additional pressure on us to be able to do that.

Leadership turbulence and trust

Of course, that's not the end of our challenges as leaders. There are also specific challenges in the leadership space that will impact our context.

The *World Economic Forum Future of Jobs Report 2023* estimates that over the next five years, 44% of workers' skills will be disrupted by the rapid increase in the importance of cognitive skills driven by the need for complex problem-solving.[6] However, leaders today recognise that they're likely not going to be able to meet that need. Organisations surveyed identified that skills gaps and an inability to attract talent would stymie industry transformation.[7]

If we want to be able to adapt to this wave of transformation as leaders we will need to focus on attracting and growing talent, building redundancy and resiliency into our teams and organisations while simultaneously developing agility and the capability to shift quickly. A big ask.

---

5   Global Risks Report 2024.

6   World Economic Forum. (May 2023). 'The Future of Jobs Report 2023 [Insight Report].' https://www.weforum.org/publications/the-future-of-jobs-report-2023/.

7   World Economic Forum. Future of Jobs Report 2023.

The Edelman Trust Barometer adds yet another dimension to this tumult. The annual survey conducted since 2000 by Edelman, a global communications firm, measures the public's trust in four key institutions: government, business, media and non-governmental organisations (NGOs). The survey is based on responses from thousands of respondents across multiple countries and demographic groups.

The 2024 survey suggests:

- Many believe innovation is poorly managed and science needs better messaging, transparency and relatable explanations to improve public understanding.

- Expected rapid innovations may worsen trust issues, causing societal instability and political polarisation, with people doubting the government's ability to adequately regulate innovation.

- However, public acceptance increases where there is confidence that innovation will lead to a better future.

- Business is trusted most to introduce safe, understandable and accessible innovations, but it still sits below 60% trust.

- Trust in global companies is decreasing, with growing concern over societal threats and leaders that mislead.[8]

---

8   Edelman Trust Barometer (2024). Global Report. Online Fieldwork in 28 Countries. https://www.edelman.com/trust/2024/trust-barometer.

The future may be a super storm

The last decade has been one of turbulence punctuated by decreasing leadership trust. But unfortunately, the future doesn't look to be one of less change – in fact, the opposite is true. If this past decade was a storm, the next one may well be a super storm due to the change on the horizon.

Indications are that this decade will be more volatile with more extreme economic swings due to the impact of innovation, workforce challenges and geo-political shifts, and the next decade presents more threats. Some of these might be increasing cyber threats, struggles with talent management and shifts in labour expectations, disruptive innovations and heightened regulatory changes and scrutiny.[9]

The coming decade is also expected to bring opportunities that can be leveraged, like generative AI, providing more time for creativity and helping to challenge conventional thinking on a broader scale, assuming the expected problems can be mitigated. But managing these new opportunities is, again, another layer of challenge.

---

9   Global Risks Report 2024; Moore, M. (18 July 2024). 'Top Business Risks for the Next Decade.' Risk Management Magazine. https://www.rmmagazine.com/articles/article/2024/07/18/top-business-risks-for-the-next-decade; Harris, K et al. (7 February 2018). 'Labor 2030: The Collision of Demographics, Automation and Inequality.' [Report]. Bain & Company. https://www.bain.com/insights/labor-2030-the-collision-of-demographics-automation-and-inequality/#:~:text=Demographics,%20automation%20and%20inequality%20have%20the; (24 August 2023). '2023 Intergenerational Report.' [Report]. Australian Government. https://treasury.gov.au/publication/2023-intergenerational-report; (30 April 2023). 'The Future of Jobs Report 2023.' World Economic Forum. https://www.weforum.org/publications/the-future-of-jobs-report-2023/in-full/1-introduction-the-global-labour-market-landscape-in-2023/; (23 January 2023). 'What is the future of work?' McKinsey & Company. https://www.mckinsey.com/featured-insights/mckinsey-explainers/what-is-the-future-of-work.

This combination of turbulence and the rising lack of trust in leadership will make our global context even more challenging. We will need more leaders who can ride these storms, making it even more crucial that leaders are aware of and mind the shadows they cast as leaders.

Leaders could also find themselves facing additional local challenges such as:

- Greater workforce disruptions than those expected as people leave in search of more stable and transparent environments.

- Teams afraid to share novel ideas or take calculated risks.

- Communication breakdowns that result in the hoarding, misunderstanding or distortion of critical information.

- People making hasty, ill-considered decisions based on limited or misleading information, perpetuating a cycle of bad outcomes.

- Diversion of people's energy to defensive behaviours and office politics that would be better directed toward achieving goals.

- Amplification of the effects of emergent crises because lack of trust exacerbates the turbulence.

- Clients or customers losing confidence in the organisation's ability to deliver consistent quality and service.

- Splintered teams that work against rather than with each other.

- Reputational damage that deters future talent and business partnerships and stalls careers.[10]

---

10 Global Risks Report 2024; Moore. Top Business Risks for the Next Decade; Harris. Labor 2030; 2023 Intergenerational Report; The Future of Jobs Report 2023; What is the future of work?

Management scholar Peter Drucker said,

'The greatest danger in times of turbulence is not the turbulence itself, but to act with yesterday's logic.'[11]

But if yesterday's logic is like a game of chess where skilled players think several moves ahead, not just reacting but proactively planning their game, then the next decade will be like playing 4D chess, simultaneously balancing multiple, layered considerations.

It's no longer enough to be able to play a single game on one board. Leaders will need to be able to simultaneously and flexibly respond in new ways to these rapidly increasing people challenges, economic shifts, social issues and technological changes.

As a skilled (leadership) chess player, you'll need to have an endgame in mind, working backward to align your current moves with a longer-term strategy. However, that vision for the future is more about the direction and journey than a specific destination, given you'll be navigating through significant periods of uncertainty.

11 McConnell, J. (30 September 2020). 'Leadership Everywhere Means Reversed Leadership.' 16th Global Peter Drucker Forum 2024. https://www.druckerforum.org/blog/leadership-everywhere-means-reversed-leadership-by-jane-mcconnell/.

History shows us change is accelerating

Add to this turbulence and diminishing trust the accelerating pace of change. In the modern era, we've moved from slow, steady, linear change to exponential change.

Let's go back in time to a small, artisanal workshop where a lone craftsman is meticulously fashioning a leather harness. It's 1837, and the world is largely predictable. Linear change and growth are the norm.

Over time, the workshop gains a reputation for making the finest horse harnesses and carriage accoutrements. The craftsman continues to innovate and develop the design and quality of his harnesses, winning multiple awards, including first prize at the 1867 World's Fair in Paris.[12]

That artisan leaves a highly profitable harness business servicing the nobility and carriage businesses to his grandsons. When city officials decide the street that houses the business is too narrow to accommodate the growth in traffic, the grandsons move locations and begin to sell their saddlery to the public for the first time. Their clientele expands beyond the nobility to other people with money.

In 1900, their saddlery line expands to include a specially designed travel bag. At the time, it was revolutionary. Its robust construction and practicality made it a travel game changer. The design is remarkably like the bags they produce today, in other words, it's stood the test of time.

---

12   (7 April 2023). 'Company History Hermès.' Wunderlabel. https://wunderlabel.com/lab/
      fashion-company-histories/hermes/.

In the aftermath of World War I, the need for horses and carriages changed. The family business shifts from making leather harnesses to crafting luxury car accessories. They survive the disruption and continue to thrive.

The family business innovates again by introducing the zipper to France and continues to expand its physical presence and range in the 1920s and 1930s.[13] They move beyond European markets to the United States. They partner with Swiss watchmakers to sell timepieces and, in 1949, launch their fragrance line.

Post-war affluence brings an increased demand for luxury items. They capitalise on this, introducing products like silk scarves and a wider range of leather bags. These begin to set fashion trends across the globe eventually becoming iconic in the fashion industry. However, with this expansion comes complexity – unexpected challenges with sourcing materials, managing international logistics and maintaining quality.

In the 1960s and 70s their competitors latch onto new opportunities and begin to use newly developed technologically engineered materials like nylon, polyester and vinyl. With the increased competition the business goes into decline. Their former competitive edge, the quality of their craft and materials, loses its shine.

They adapt again, reducing their focus to three core product lines – ready-wear, silk scarves and leather goods. They use insights about customer problems and experiment with bag designs that result in significant commercial success, with their products often passed from generation to generation.

In the 1990s, they capitalise on the emergence of supermodels and celebrity fashion and shift focus to their ready-to-wear fashion lines. They restrict

---

13   Company History Hermès.

supply to increase exclusivity and create greater demand for their bag lines, making them highly profitable and seeing the business growing again.

Then comes the digital age. The pace of change is no longer linear; it's become exponential. The age of instant information and consumer reviews threatens the traditional approaches that sustained them for decades. They must invest in cutting-edge technology, digitise their customer experience and adopt data analytics to understand emerging consumer trends and opportunities. And they must do it quickly.

They create more consumer barriers, making accessing their exclusive products more desirable by making them harder for consumers to buy. They adopt sustainable practices and leverage the timelessness and quality of their products with a network of repair workshops that preserve the sustainability of their products. In 2023 alone, their workshops restored 200,000 products.[14] Profits are reinvested back into the business and in 2023 revenue exceeded €13 billion.[15]

In 2023, the business that started in 1837 as a small, artisanal workshop with a lone craftsman had 294 stores,[16] 60 production sites and 22,000 employees operating globally.[17]

So far, Hermès has more than weathered almost two centuries of challenges, proving that even in a world where change is the only constant, ingenuity and adaptability can stand the test of time. But the pace at which those challenges are emerging is only going to increase.

<hr>

14 'Sustainable Development.' Hermès Paris. https://www.hermes.com/au/en/ content/134986-sustainable-development/.

15 'Total revenue of Hermès worldwide 2007-2023.' Statista. https://www.statista.com/ statistics/245917/total-revenue-of-hermes-worldwide/.

16 Sabanoglu, T. (4 April 2024). 'Global number of Hermès stores 2007-2023.' Statista. https://www.statista.com/statistics/245931/number-of-hermes-stores-worldwide/.

17 'Activity Report 2023.' Hermès Paris. https://assets-finance.hermes.com/s3fs-public/ node/pdf_file/2024-04/1713264064/hermes_20240416_2023activityreport_en.pdf.

Sustainability and climate change present more complex challenges as Hermès works to reduce emissions impact across the supply chain. Unfortunately for Hermès, leather goods make up more than half of their revenue, and cattle generate 40% of the world's methane[18], a greenhouse gas 28% more damaging to the climate than carbon dioxide.[19]

Where there was once plenty of time to experiment and adapt, Hermès, like all other organisations and the people who lead them, must learn to adapt to multiple challenges simultaneously.

In the 1960s, American engineer Gordon Moore, who co-founded Fairchild Semiconductor and later Intel, said that the number of transistors on an integrated circuit would reach 65,000 by 1975. In 1975 he updated his prediction to say that the number of transistors on a single circuit would double every two years while the cost would halve over the same period. His prediction became a general self-fulfilling prophecy for digital electronics and is now known as Moore's Law.[20]

Futurist Ray Kurzweil predicts that we'll see the equivalent of a century of progress in a quarter of the time it now takes to double the rate of progress. But we're rapidly reaching the stage where predictions will become meaningless. Kurzweil's Law of Accelerating Returns implies that the pace of technological evolution will reach a speed at which future change will be

---

18 Booker, C & Weber, S. (6 March 2022). 'Cow burps are a major contributor to climate change – can scientists change that?' [Audio.] PBS News Weekend. https://www.pbs.org/newshour/show/cow-burps-are-a-major-contributor-to-climate-change-can-scientists-change-that.

19 (1 November 2023). 'Importance of methane.' Global Methane Initiative. United States Environmental Protection Agency. https://www.epa.gov/gmi/importance-methane#:~:text=Methane%20is%20more%20than%2028,due%20to%20human%2Drelated%20activities..

20 Tardi, C. (2 April 2024). 'What Is Moore's Law and Is It Still True?' Investopedia. https://www.investopedia.com/terms/m/mooreslaw.asp.

impossible to predict.[21] This means we can no longer rely on past estimates about the rate of change when making plans for the future.

The growth in internet users since the late eighties is an example of how technological change is accelerating over time. In October 2023, there were an estimated 5.4 billion users, a quadrupling of users since 2005.[22] And the rate of growth is continuing to accelerate. Current estimates put users at an estimated 7.3 billion by 2029.[23] And this growth isn't limited to internet usage. Consider the release of ChatGPT, which surpassed one million users within five days of its release.[24]

Kurzweil talks about how the trend line associated with technological growth is becoming increasingly vertical as can be seen with the rapid and unconstrained emergence and uptake of generative AI between late 2022 and mid-2023. He believes we are moving towards 'the singularity' – a transforming event that will occur in the first half of the 21st century where 'the pace of technological change will be so rapid, its impact so deep, that human life will be irreversibly transformed'.[25]

He estimates that 'by the end of this century, the nonbiological portion of our intelligence will be trillions of trillions of times more powerful than unaided human intelligence'.

21   Buchanan, M. (July 2008). 'The law of accelerating returns.' Nature Physics. https://www.nature.com/articles/nphys1010.

22   (2024). 'Number of internet users worldwide from 2005 to 2023.' Statista. https://www.statista.com/statistics/273018/number-of-internet-users-worldwide/.

23   Law, D. (5 March 2024). 'Australian Internet Statistics 2024.' Red Search. https://www.redsearch.com.au/resources/australian-internet-statistics/#:~:text=Internet%20Statistics%20Forecast%20for%202024,a%20new%20peak%20by%202029.

24   'ChatGPT Statistics: Rapid Growth from Launch to 2023-2024.' WiserNotify. https://wisernotify.com/blog/chatgpt-users/#:~:text=Launched%20in%20November%202022%2C%20ChatGPT,fastest%2Dgrowing%20applications%20in%20history..

25   Kurzweil, R. (2024). *The Singularity is Nearer: When We Merge with AI*. Jonathan Cape & BH – Trade.

It helps to visualise this if you imagine slowly pouring milk into a cup of coffee. At the singularity, it's as if someone knocked the milk you are pouring and the entire bottle of milk splashes in at once, completely overwhelming the coffee.

Whether the singularity happens or not, it's inarguable that the pace of change is rapidly accelerating. When we combine this with the broad range of expected changes, it's reasonable to expect we'll need to navigate converging storm fronts.

Learning to navigate the storm

Unless we're able to centre ourselves as leaders, we may find those converging storm fronts, i.e. the context, is all we can see. Centring yourself is vital as the context is constantly evolving.

As humans we tend to organise what we see and experience in a way that helps us make sense of how the world works. This is known as the 'perceptual process'.[26] Not only do we place our own interpretations on what we see, hear and experience, we also gravitate towards what helps us make sense of what is happening around us.

There are some concepts that help us to better understand what we are perceiving in the storms that surround us. And the first of these is what is known as VUCA.

---

26   https://opentextbc.ca/introconsumerbehaviour/chapter/the-perceptual-process/

VUCA

To start to understand VUCA, let's go back to 2001.

I was sitting in my parents' lounge room, watching in horror as the television broadcasted images of planes flying into the side of the World Trade Centre and the Pentagon in the US. My three-year-old son came running down the hallway, stopped, looked at the television and started laughing.

Now my son isn't a psychopath! He just had no idea that what he was seeing on the television was horribly real. He thought it was make-believe play, like when he crashed his toy plane into a tower of blocks that he had piled up, one on top of the other. And to be honest, it almost didn't seem real to me – or to many of us around the world. Up until that day, commercial planes purposefully flying into the sides of skyscrapers were not real.

What happened on 9/11 woke the world up to a stark reality – conventional military and strategic planning approaches were insufficient.

The emergence of clandestine cells of resistance fighters during conflicts between nation-states was not new. We knew what terrorist cells were in the years before 9/11. However, the way in which those cells were emerging and operating on a global stage changed how nation-states needed to respond.

The attacks showcased how threats could be unconventional and unpredictable and expanded our awareness of military and strategic frameworks to help us make more sense of a VUCA world.

The acronym 'VUCA' was originally coined by the U.S. Army War College in the late 1980s and published by Herbert Barber in 1992.[27] It stands for and

---

27   Barber, H.F. (1992), 'Developing Strategic Leadership: The US Army War College Experience', Journal of Management Development, Vol. 11 No. 6, pp. 4-12. https://doi. org/10.1108/02621719210018208.

describes the volatility, uncertainty, complexity and ambiguity (VUCA) of modern warfare and global dynamics. The methodology around VUCA was developed from concepts presented by leadership experts Warren Bennis and Burt Nanus in their book *Leaders: The Strategies for Taking Charge.*[28]

While VUCA had been discussed in military circles prior to 9/11, the terrorist attacks accelerated the adoption of its methodology across various sectors, underscoring the need for new strategies that could operate effectively under such turbulent conditions.

In this new VUCA world, linear planning models proved obsolete. Adaptive leadership, agile strategy formulation and resilience became the new cornerstones for military – and later business – strategies.

This paradigm shift didn't just change military tactics; it permeated corporate boardrooms, public policy forums and leadership think tanks, all seeking to navigate a world that had suddenly become much more VUCA. And when COVID-19 emerged in 2020, each component – volatility, uncertainty, complexity and ambiguity – was magnified in unprecedented ways.

The VUCA Framework

- **Volatile**

  When the novel coronavirus emerged, it was **volatile**. It spread like wildfire, affecting millions within weeks, sending parts of the economy into freefall and putting already stressed health systems under even more stress.

  Governments and organisations had to pivot rapidly, often within hours, as new information became available. Traditional forecasting

---

28   Bennis, W & Nanus, B. (2003). *Leaders: Strategies for Taking Charge.* Collins Business Essentials.

models crumbled under the erratic nature of the pandemic's spread and socio-economic impact.

- **Uncertain**

  The future was **uncertain** despite an onslaught of research about the virus's origins, characteristics and long-term impacts. Strategies that seemed effective one moment were questioned the next, making it incredibly difficult for leaders to make well-informed decisions.

- **Complex**

  The pandemic was a **complexity** of crises layered and intersecting with each other. It was a health, economic, social and geopolitical crisis all rolled into one. It necessitated multidisciplinary, multi-sectoral and industry solutions involving public health experts, economists, social scientists and geopolitical analysts.

- **Ambiguous**

  Ambiguity reigned supreme. Conflicting reports, misinformation and the absence of a recent, historical playbook (the Spanish influenza pandemic was in 1918) added vagueness to an already convoluted situation. Leaders had to make high-stakes decisions with **ambiguous** and often incomplete information.

COVID-19 exemplified the VUCA world, challenging traditional models of leadership and strategy and compelling organisations and governments to adapt, innovate and be resilient in the face of profound instability. And many more people in wide-ranging industries across the globe grasped the concept of VUCA to help them make sense of what was happening in their world. But it's not limited to just the pandemic. VUCA is here to stay.

You can also think of a VUCA world in these ways:

Imagine you're on a ship sailing at sea. There's a gentle breeze pushing you along. Then, seemingly out of nowhere, you're amid a storm. Then just as suddenly the storm is gone, taking all the wind with it, and you're sitting in a dead calm.

Or, as you jump on the roller coaster at a theme park, the attendant blindfolds you. You feel the carriage climbing upwards. You know it will drop at some point, but you don't know when. Suddenly, you're flying downwards, and unexpectedly, the carriage pulls to the left, then sharp to the right – you didn't see it coming. **That's volatility.**

Now, you're in a car driving down a winding road. It's the middle of the night, and you're surrounded by fog. You can only see immediately in front of you, and it's hard to predict what will happen next.

Or you arrive at a restaurant where you're having a gourmet meal except the restaurant is pitch black. You know the food on the end of your fork is edible, but you don't know if you'll like the taste or texture. All you can do is take a bite and hope for the best. **That's uncertainty.**

We all know how hard it is to herd cats but imagine if you were asked to teach them synchronised swimming. You have multiple individuals, all with their own personalities and perspectives, and you need to find a way to get them to move forward together in sync while the kids in the 'learn to swim' class next door keep throwing their toys into the next pool, distracting the cats.

Or, after a very frustrating day teaching cats, you must cook a three-course gourmet feast. The catch is you need to use recipes written in five different languages. There are many crucial elements, and you are constantly making sense and adjusting your actions to avoid an inedible mess. However, it's hard to fully grasp how to combine all elements to provide a pleasing experience. **That's complexity.**

You asked your teenage son to let you know his plans for the weekend. He sent you a text message outlining his plans, except it's a long string of emojis with multiple meanings. You have no idea what it means or if that's his plan for Saturday, Sunday or the whole weekend.

The next day, you're at a Chinese restaurant with your partner, having a conversation about your next career move. You decide to put your fate in the hands of a fortune cookie. You crack the cookie in half, pull out the paper, and stare perplexed at the message 'Adventure Awaits!'. Does that mean you're about to go overseas on a holiday, you will move to a new role or your partner has bought you a tandem skydive for your birthday? **That's ambiguity.**

BANI

VUCA is just one conceptual framework or lens through which we can view our changing world and focus our understanding. On April 30, 2020, futurist James Cascio released a blog on *Medium* that presented another perspective.[29]

Cascio declared we live in an age of chaos and that given the inadequacy of existing tools to recognise and respond to disruption, we needed 'a new method or tool to see the shapes this age of chaos takes.' His view was that as VUCA had become a default condition, it was not telling us anything new or offering previously unseen insights. Instead, he proposed a new perspective, BANI.

---

29   Cascio, J. (30 April 2020). 'Facing the Age of Chaos.' *Medium*. https://medium.
com/@cascio/facing-the-age-of-chaos-b00687b1f51d.

The BANI framework

- **Brittle**
- **Anxious**
- **Nonlinear**
- **Incomprehensible**

Cascio's BANI framework provides a different lens through which we can understand what's happening in our world. But how is BANI different to VUCA?

Imagine your life as a smartphone. In a VUCA world, your phone's battery drains faster than usual, apps freeze now and then and sometimes you lose signal. However, in a BANI world, your smartphone is overheating, spam notifications are flooding in, apps are crashing left and right and you can't even figure out how to turn the device off. The upheaval and changes are exponentially multiplied. That is the level of complexity and stress Cascio talks about.

He sees the world as going through a phase shift, where, like when you heat water and it turns to steam, it's essentially changing form. This is an exponential change that demands a new way of thinking to allow us explore, make sense of and respond to it, rather than simply react to what is happening.

So why does Cascio believe the upheavals we see in the world are multiplying rather than just adding to our stress?

The meaning behind the words in the letters that make up BANI provide further insight.

Brittle

In a brittle world, the systems and institutions around us are not as strong as we assume and are liable to break or snap easily under stress or pressure. It's like walking on a frozen pond that might crack any minute – it looks strong until it's not. When things that are brittle fail, they shatter, often with catastrophic consequences.

Think of the many businesses that failed during the pandemic and subsequent financial pressures due to the compounding stressors of government restrictions, supply chain failures, workforce constraints, scarcity-driven price rises and changes in consumer demand. Failure happens because of the reliance on single, critical points in systems without built-in slack.

Our hyper-connected world means the impact of what might have been a crisis in one region or country can quickly spread globally. Like the ice on a frozen pond, it doesn't just crack in one place. It sends cracks and weaknesses throughout the entire body of water.

Anxious

Cascio suggests that this brittleness in our world induces anxiety. Today people – including leaders – are constantly on edge. We feel like we're waiting for the other shoe to drop but have no idea when or where it will happen.

Do you remember how many people were glued to their televisions or doom scrolling on their phones for the next broadcast about the latest infection hot spot, numbers of COVID-19 cases and country-by-country death tolls throughout the pandemic? Or how many conspiracy theorists and anti-vaxxers suddenly popped up on your Facebook news feed, presenting their beliefs as facts? And do you remember the heightened anxiety that brought into your life? It was real, and physical, and felt across the world.

The anxiety led to a rapid realisation of how much is outside our control – not that it ever was. The impact of this was a desire by many to blame 'those people' secretly pulling the strings. But we also saw a significant increase in mental health disorders, including a rapid rise in suicide rates.[30]

Anxiety because things were outside of our control simply came to a head – came into visibility – because of COVID, but it's always been there. And Cascio said this is increasing.

Nonlinear

In complexity, hindsight often helps us make the links between cause and effect – if that is even possible. However, with BANI, the non-linearity is even more disconnected and disproportionate. Things do not follow a straightforward path, and a small change in one part of a system can lead to exponential impacts elsewhere. In some ways this is like the butterfly effect, the idea that where a butterfly flapping its wings in India causes a cyclone here in Australia. But that still has a linear structure. Instead, non-linearity is like a butterfly flapping its wings in India and cows learning to fly in Australia. The links between cause and effect – however tenuous they were in the first place – seem almost completely nonsensical.

And the consequences may not manifest immediately. There may be lengthy delays between the occurrence and the impact – think climate change. The reasons for the impact may also be impossible to understand... which takes us to our final point.

---

30   Brunier, A & Drysdale. C. (2 March 2022). 'COVID-19 pandemic triggers 25% increase in prevalence of anxiety and depression worldwide: Wake-up call to all countries to step up mental health services and support.' World Health Organization. https://www.who.int/news/item/02-03-2022-covid-19-pandemic-triggers-25-increase-in-prevalence-of-anxiety-and-depression-worldwide.

Incomprehensible

Cascio argues we have moved from ambiguous, where there could be multiple meanings, to flat out incomprehensible. He believes that with incomprehensibility, we're trying to understand why and how things happen, but the answers don't make sense. Instead, we become overwhelmed by information overload where we cannot explain exactly why things like computer algorithms do and don't work when we make a change.

And we're coming to the realisation that machine learning is picking up more than what we would prefer it learns, such as the bias that drives outcomes in the real world.[31]

Various studies have shown that predictive models are inaccurate for minorities and other groups deserving of equity.[32] Although machines are learning, they are often not accompanied by analysis that detects bias. And so bias occurs. And with bias comes information that is inaccurate, adding more obstructions to the comprehensibility.

The reasons behind non-linear impacts may be impossible to understand now (i.e., incomprehensible), but we'll eventually figure it out and then we must deal with the inevitable consequences. That is more volatility, more brittleness, more uncertainty, more anxiety... more complexity.

---

31   'Fairness: Types of Bias.' [Online course.] Crash Course: Machine Learning. Google for Developers Newsletter. https://developers.google.com/machine-learning/crash-course/fairness/types-of-bias.

32   Jindal, A. (5 September 2022). 'Misguided Artificial Intelligence: How Racial Bias is Built Into Clinical Models.' *Brown Hospital Medicine.* https://bhm.scholasticahq.com/article/38021-misguided-artificial-intelligence-how-racial-bias-is-built-into-clinical-models.

VUCA vs BANI

I don't believe VUCA has passed its use-by date. Every situation is different, and one event, like a pandemic, does not change the characteristics of all things that exist and happen. However, it's clear that VUCA does not encapsulate everything we need to help us navigate the storm of constant change.

Cascio suggested BANI hints at opportunities for how we should respond or at least initially react. For example, we could:

- Meet brittleness with resilience and slack.
- Ease anxiety with empathy and mindfulness.
- Use context and flexibility in nonlinearity.
- Rally against incomprehensibility with transparency and intuition.[33]

Both VUCA and BANI help us make sense of the constantly-emerging challenges in our world. Both are essential to helping us understand how we can approach our reality.

But, regrettably, they also leave a lot unsaid about managing ourselves in that context. And that is the gap that this book seeks to address.

As you read this book, remember the saying:

'It is not the strongest species that survive, nor the most intelligent, but the ones who are most responsive to change'.

This quote is wise advice in a VUCA world. It's often erroneously attributed to Charles Darwin, but is generally attributed to Leon C. Megginson, a

---

33 Cascio. Facing the Age of Chaos.

Professor at Louisiana State University during the 1960s.[34] Megginson talked about Darwin's ideas on evolution in a speech he gave on adapting to change within the business environment. He used Darwin's theory of natural selection to show that adaptability is key if you want to survive in the business world as much as in the natural world.[35]

Leadership in the eye of the storm

So, as leaders, we don't need to be the strongest – or the most intelligent. We need to be the most responsive to change to survive the storm that we're in. And to do that, we need to centre our leadership. We need to find the eye of the storm.

Think of the world as a giant mobile hanging from the ceiling, with each country, innovation and political shift represented by a different piece. When one piece moves, it sets off a chain reaction that causes the entire mobile to sway and shift.

As individual leaders, we're like the delicate ornaments hanging from the bottom of the mobile. Even the smallest movement at the top can create ripples that reach us, making us sway in ways we never anticipated. Our challenge is to find balance amidst the motion, and ways to adapt to the new rhythms created by the global dance.

The risk if we don't? Leadership burnout and organisational failure. And we've got to address the first to stop the second.

---

34   Darwin Correspondent Project. 'The evolution of a misquotation.' University of Cambridge. https://www.darwinproject.ac.uk/people/about-darwin/six-things-darwin-never-said/ evolution-misquotation#:~:text=Megginson%20wrote%20in%201963%3A,in%20which%20 it%20finds%20itself.

35   Darwin Correspondent Project. The evolution of a misquotation.

My burnout was 15 years in the making. 15 years where the pace of change was undoubtedly rapid, but slower than what we can expect in the future. So how are we going to avoid igniting into burnout in this environment of rapidly increasing change?

Imagine the stormy seas once again. Envision the torrential rain, the howling winds, and the relentless waves. The storm is generated by the interaction between different elements influencing your context and the interaction between you and that context. It can feel chaotic, disorienting and overwhelming. But, as any seasoned sailor will tell you, even the fiercest storm has an eye – a calm centre.

This book is an invitation to learn how to move from the tumult of the storm to its tranquil centre and practice leadership in the eye of the storm.

It's about understanding the storm, respecting its power, and leveraging your own.

This book is not merely words on paper. It seeks to help you find a more tranquil centre at the eye of the storm from which you can make better sense of, respond to and even harness that change.

Centring is not about staying in the eye permanently. That simply won't happen. It's about finding the eye, taking the next step or action to further your organisation and leadership and, just as you're facing more volatility and upheaval, coming back to the eye, again and then again and then again.

I invite you to treat this book as a tool for navigation. We'll learn how to find your way to the eye of the storm by using the Centring Star and tethering it to your inner compass so you can move from feeling lost in the storm to becoming the storm's master.

We'll dissect how the shadows we cast as leaders can be amplified during perfect storms. We'll explore the value of deeply grounding ourselves in the present, and how by centring ourselves in the eye of the storm we can sense-make and conduct ourselves in ways that serve us and the people and organisations we lead.

We'll draw upon proven frameworks for navigating that complexity and the evidence about building a tolerance of ambiguity to experience higher performance and well-being.

And we'll also shine a spotlight on the emotional anchors that, often unbeknownst to us, hold us back and drag us under that perfect storm. Most importantly, we'll work our way through the Centring Star methodology so you can move from a place of fear, being overwhelmed and at risk of burnout to a space where you inspire trust, drive meaningful change and experience sustainable success in alignment with your core values and beliefs.

Louisa May Alcott, one of my favourite childhood authors, summed up the journey this book will take you on when she wrote:

'I am not afraid of storms, for I am learning how to sail my ship.'

Let's go learn how to sail our ship.

PART 2

WHAT HOLDS
YOU BACK

CHAPTER 2

Anchored in Yesterday

*'To reach a port, we must sail – sail, not
tie at anchor – sail, not drift.'*
Franklin D. Roosevelt

In a world that constantly urges us forward, that's in a constant state of flux with layers of complexity, the idea of being anchored in yesterday reflects the subtle but significant ways that we allow our past – whether those are successes in our work, or the storms that we just didn't see coming – to serve as shackles, binding us to outdated methods, giving us misplaced confidence and keeping us in the confusion and disruption of the storm.

This quote by President Roosevelt is our call to action, urging us to move beyond the comfortable confines of the past, even including our previous victories, and embrace future opportunities, both professionally and personally. It is only when we let go of the past that we can be fully centred leaders.

So, what does hold us back from moving out of the storm and becoming centred leaders?

The problem with being successful

Success is great. Being successful is generally our goal as leaders in any organisation. But success without understanding why we're successful can lead to more problems in the future.

In 2003, as Ducati was taking its first turn on the MotoGP track, the Ducati team approached the season with a learner's mindset, preparing to gain more insights than trophies. But as they began racking up podium finishes, their narrative and expectations shifted.

When the 2004 season began, success quietly turned from an ally to an adversary. And they didn't notice until it was too late. The team started the 2004 season with expectations that their high performance and success would continue as it had in the previous year. Those expectations were quickly dashed when previously unrecognised design flaws impacted their performance.

They couldn't effectively respond when things started going wrong because they didn't understand why they'd been successful in the first place. Because risks had not manifested during their previous success, they assumed those risks simply didn't exist.

When Filippo Preziosi from the Ducati Corse team was asked to reflect on what happened, he said, 'In racing, when you make a change, you only care whether or not it leads to superior performance. You tend to care less why something works. But over the long term you need to know why. This is the science.'[36]

---

36   Gino, F & Pisano, G. (2011). 'Why Leaders Don't Learn from Success.' *Harvard Business Review*. https://hbr.org/2011/04/why-leaders-dont-learn-from-success.

Preziosi had realised a common trap we can all fall into: we like to focus on what went right rather than what went wrong. Who wouldn't rather celebrate a win than spend time considering why we won and whether it was because of our innate talent or because the stars happened to align at that exact point in time so we could perform at our best?

Tales like Ducati's do not only happen on racetracks. It is not uncommon for past triumphs to lead us astray.

Harvard researchers Francesca Gino and Gary Pisano reviewed Ducati's experience and found that their success masked the very elements that forged it.[37] The resulting complacency undercut Ducati's future success, and the same can happen to any organisation.

When things work, it's not always because we know what we're doing. Maybe we just got lucky and didn't know it. Unfortunately, those same conditions may not exist the next time, which means the same approach won't work either. It's akin to using a GPS that only shows the last turn you made correctly, but not the full journey ahead. You simply can't see why you're getting anywhere – and because of that, you can't replicate the good decisions and choices that saw you succeeding.

The downside of success is it doesn't motivate us to revise our theories or expand our knowledge. Things worked, so why question it? We're more likely to conclude that our talents and our current strategy are the reasons we were successful. And so, we tend to ignore the part that environmental factors and random events played in our success.

Gino and Pisano did more research in different fields like software, medicine and entertainment, to see why today's success can lead to future failures. They ran tests in the lab and with executives, and despite different industries

---

37   Gino. Ducati Corse: The Making of a Grand Prix Motorcycle..

and challenges, they found four things that make it harder to learn when you are successful regardless of industry. These are attribution bias, escalation of commitment, complacency and overconfidence.[38]

1. Attribution bias

The first part of the pattern is that as humans we tend to think that other people's success is due to luck and outside factors, not leadership skills. We have trouble seeing how the situation might have affected the choices that people made.

Gino and Pisano saw that drug company managers thought that their project got funded because of the high quality of their science team. They didn't realise that other projects, with equally high-quality science teams, didn't get funding simply because the company was not competitive in those markets. The researchers also saw that the success of new drugs, which can take a long time to launch, was still typically credited to the current strategy, management and scientists, not to what happened before, despite the 'before' work being the real pillars of the current success.[39]

2. Escalation of commitment

Success can lead us to overcommit to our current strategy or promise. We see that it's worked in the past and we want to replicate that success – so we hold tightly onto what we're already doing. This makes it difficult to adapt or change when the situation adapts or changes, or when the goal posts move.

---

38   Gino. Why Leaders Don't Learn from Success.
39   Gino. Why Leaders Don't Learn from Success.

3. Complacency

Achieving success can create a false sense of security within our leadership. This reduces our own motivation to innovate, make changes, adapt or address emerging challenges. Change is hard. It takes time and energy and resources. So, when things seem to be working, it's human nature to stay the course. Unfortunately, complacency stops us from looking forward and, as we've seen, this undermines future successes, particularly in a world that's growing more complex.

4. Leadership overconfidence

Another problem the researchers found is that the executives they studied from different industries had too much confidence.[40] Those who remembered being successful were more likely to take bigger risks because they believed in their skills, expected more success in the future, thought they knew everything they needed and believed that their plans and procedures were working.

However, success does not have to lead to complacency or overconfidence. When Steve Jobs acquired the computer division from Lucasfilm and helped found a new company called Pixar in 1986, no one expected its phenomenal success. That's because before Pixar emerged, the commercial success of computer-animated movies was hugely inconsistent. It was uncommon for a production company to have a series of hits, let alone more than 10 consecutively.[41]

---

40 Gino. Why Leaders Don't Learn from Success.

41 Rengel, A. (17 April 2021). 'How Pixar Makes Movies Everyone Loves.' *Medium.* https://
ajrengel-75816.medium.com/how-pixar-makes-movies-everyone-loves-17d82f9469de.

What made Pixar different was its readiness to use post-mortems to examine why it was successful.[42] Ed Catmull, who led Pixar as President for 33 years, did not allow them to fall into the trap of relying on their past achievements. Catmull's insistence on rigorous post-mortems, regardless of a movie's success or failure, contributed to Pixar's long series of hits.[43] And it worked.

After studying the experiences of Ducati, Pixar and many other executive leaders, Gino and Pisano advise us to 'use success to breed more success by understanding it.'[44] We can't simply rest on our laurels when we're experiencing success as leaders or within our organisation. We can't remain anchored in the past. Because this will ultimately lead to failure.

Captured by stories

We accumulate stories in our lives that shape our identities over time, both personally and as leaders. And sometimes these stories become a drag (or an anchor!) on our ability to get out of the storm and into more centred leadership.

My background is more working class than middle class, but I was always encouraged to be the best I could be. My dad had to leave school as soon as he could to earn money and help the family. His first job was at Busby's. They cleaned used 'tallies', the tall brown beer bottles, for the XXXX (Fourex) beer factory in Brisbane. Over time, he leveraged that job into running his own recycling business, and this was before sustainability even became a trend.

Going to work with dad during the school holidays was fun for me and my brother. We'd sit next to him on the front seat of his big red International

---

42 Catmull, E. (2008). 'How Pixar Fosters Collective Creativity.' *Harvard Business Review.* https://hbr.org/2008/09/how-pixar-fosters-collective-creativity.

43 Catmull. How Pixar Fosters Collective Creativity.

44 Gino. Why Leaders Don't Learn from Success.

Prime Mover truck, driving between Boy Scout dens and pubs, to pick up the bottles. We'd run along the back of the long semi-trailer, helping him load the tallies people had gathered to raise funds into the truck, and jump back in for the ride to return them to Busby's.

My dad worked very long hours, leaving well before sunrise. And on the days that he travelled further north and south, he didn't come back until late at night. He worked extremely hard, but change comes despite hard work no matter what industry you're in. So, when tallies started to be replaced by stubbies (shorter beer bottles), dad had to make a change too. He sold the semi-trailer, bought a smaller tip truck with a crane and started collecting drums of glass for recycling from the backs of pubs, clubs and other businesses, work he did until he retired.

My dad worked a tough, physical job all his life. His business supported his family, and we had a wonderful family life. My dad's story, featuring hard work and determination, is one of the stories that shaped me as well. His story influenced my story; reverberating through my life.

My mum had a story too. Family circumstances and social norms held my mum back when it came to pursuing a career. She could not continue her high school education after her father died, due to family circumstances. When my mum married, she was made to leave her job as personal secretary to senior leaders in the Department of Education in Queensland. She found another job as secretary to the Managing Director of an international business but had to leave that when I was born. She did eventually return to that role after my younger brother started school. Over the years the fortunes of that company changed, and the Brisbane office ultimately closed. However, that didn't stop mum. She had a career break but went back as a merchandiser until she too retired. My mum's story influenced my story as well. One of perseverance and flexibility in the face of challenges and change.

My parents both had a strong work ethic. Because dad was denied more than a basic education and knew how intelligent mum was, he was committed to ensuring my brother and I had the opportunity to learn. As the eldest, I most felt the force of those expectations.

The woman I called Grandma (it's a long story) told me that from the time I was tiny my dad would bounce me on his knee and share with anyone who would listen that I was going to university. During primary school, I vividly remember sitting at the family dinner table, watching the evening news with my dad and him telling me that I would not behave like those student protestors when I went to university. The thrust is that I always understood that my story would include a university education. But these expectations also had a long-lasting impact and influenced my tendencies as a leader.

I also have a hazier recollection of being asked by my dad 'What happened?' when I came home from primary school with a report card full of As and positive teacher feedback, but punctuated with a solitary B. My parents don't remember it, but I remember how it made me feel. Like I wasn't good enough.

I suppose I felt a constant responsibility to perform and not let him down. He wasn't nasty or obnoxious about it. I knew he cared and wanted the best for me. But those expectations were a weight that drove me and influenced my behaviour and deeply-hidden anxieties.

The memory I most treasure from my first university graduation is dad telling me how proud he was that I was the first person in his family to graduate from university. It was a proud day, but perhaps I've carried that drive to achieve and meet people's expectations ever since. These stories have become deeply entwined with my identity. And they've underscored and either supported or challenged everything that I've done since that time.

I believe these stories are the source of my addiction to achievement. And because of that sometimes they've held me back and contributed to my tendency to want to please people, strive for perfection and drive myself hard to meet expectations. But stories can be like riptides, and the stories we create for ourselves can cause strong, hidden currents that impact lives when we don't realise that they're just stories.

When I work with clients, I also see stories limiting them. One client I worked with, let's call her 'Jill', subconsciously believed that she had to do everything herself in order for it to be done right. Unfortunately, this meant that she did too much herself and her team lost out on growth opportunities.

Another client, 'Jack' we'll call him, convinced himself he couldn't share his work with anyone else until he was satisfied with it. He felt too vulnerable to do so. This meant that he missed out on receiving valuable feedback and ideas from others that could have expanded his thinking and, ultimately, improved his work.

'Tom' assumed that if he was approving work, he had to be thorough and notice every detail. Unfortunately, he spent most of his time verifying information that could have been assigned to a detail-oriented team member. And because he was so bogged down with detail, he overlooked important parts of the bigger picture, which was where he should have been spending his time as a leader.

'Mary' felt that if someone asked her to do something, she had to say yes and not question why or what was most urgent right now. As a result, she constantly violated her own boundaries and suffered poor wellbeing.

These stories might feel too close for comfort – or they may not resonate with you at all. But each of us has a story that shapes how we perceive ourselves and contributes to how we act as leaders. Stories can become a habit or thinking pattern when they stem from influential periods or moments in our lives. They may have served us in those moments but can lose their usefulness over time and instead contribute to our reactive behaviours. So, our stories can have enormous power, but only if we decide to let them. And part of becoming a centred leader is to understand which of our stories help us and which don't.

When digging deep into my reactive behaviours after a significant burn out, I came across Robert Kegan and Lisa Leahy's book *Immunity to Change.*[45] Whenever I'm reading, I like to switch between hard copies and audiobooks so I can continue my 'reading' no matter where I am. I was driving one day, listening to the audiobook, when I suddenly started crying. It was one of those moments when what you hear literally clicks and unlocks something inside. I had recognised a deep part of myself in one of the stories.

When Robert Kegan was a professor at Harvard University's Graduate School of Education, he introduced groundbreaking theories on the evolution of adult consciousness.[46] Adult consciousness refers to the complex and subtle ways that adults see, analyse and engage with their environment. It integrates experiences, attitudes, values and knowledge that have been gathered across the cognitive, emotional, and social facets of our adult life. But what sets adult consciousness apart from childhood or adolescence is the potentially higher capacity of adults to self-reflect, empathise, engage in abstract thought and handle ambiguity and paradox.[47]

What's important about Kegan's work is that it offers a lens through which we can view our personal growth and the narratives that shape our identities. Kegan might tell you to imagine you're wearing glasses that colour everything

---

45 Kegan, R & Lahey, L. (2009). *Immunity to Change: How to Overcome It and Unlock the Potential in Yourself and Your Organization.* Leadership for the Common Good Series. Harvard Business Review Press.
46 Kegan. Immunity to Change.
47 Kegan. Immunity to Change.

you see. Those glasses represent the stories and beliefs we hold about ourselves. Unfortunately, those stories can sometimes be negative, unfair or harsh and we can be anchored to the past by them.

To begin to free ourselves, Kegan suggests making a subject-object shift. We can do that by imagining taking off those glasses and examining them. By removing them, we are no longer unconsciously 'subject' to the glasses' influence and can now make them an 'object' of our attention.[48]

Recognising myself in one of the case studies in the audiobook was akin to taking my glasses off. It gave me the power to question, refine, and even replace the stories I was seeing through those glasses. I began to see a person bound by her upbringing and a subconscious continuation of beliefs voiced by her parents in a completely different context. I had not realised how heavily some of my behaviours were influenced by what I had heard them say when growing up.

'As long as you know you did your best,' had turned into a harsh self-criticism about how I could have done better.

'When things get tough, you roll up your sleeves and help' made me feel like I was not being a good person unless I was also experiencing challenges alongside the people reporting to me. That may have been okay when I was an entry-level team member, but no longer served when working at the executive level.

I noticed how my subconscious thoughts differed from opinions expressed by colleagues raised in white-collar families with professional parents. Once aware of these beliefs, instead of being ensnared by them, I could assess them objectively and choose more empowering narratives.

---

48   Kegan. Immunity to Change.

It is why I now call myself a recovering perfectionist and people-pleaser. My old narrative is still there, but it loses power each time I notice one of the stories popping up and choose to behave in a way that serves today.

When we are kinder, more curious and compassionate towards ourselves, there is strong evidence stories start to lose their power, enabling us to look at situations through a different, more objective lens. It is akin to peeling the layers of an onion, gradually removing the self-limiting beliefs and narratives, one by one, until we reveal the core truth beneath all the accumulated stories.

Kristin Neff, a leading researcher and author who explores self-compassion's role in psychological well-being, says, 'To break free from self-limiting beliefs, treat yourself with the same kindness you would offer a friend.'[49]

Think of a story you often tell yourself. Now, imagine looking at it from the outside. Is it accurate? Kind? If not, how can you rewrite it in a way that's both true and supportive? What would you say to a friend with kindness? Is there anything holding you back from treating yourself with that same kindness?

You have a choice. You can cling to who you used to be, remaining anchored in your past. Or you can keep an open mind and be curious about how you behave and think and why that's tied to your sense of self.

---

49   Neff, K. (2011). *Self-Compassion: The Proven Power of Being Kind to Yourself.* William Morrow.

Pinned down by a fixed mindset

Figuring out our own stories and how these are tied into our sense of self and our sense of who we are as leaders is important, but it's not enough. You won't be in a position to adapt unless you have the courage to relax your preconceived sense of self and experiment with who you need to be next.

Researcher Carol Dweck's work on growth mindset emphasises that talents can be developed through hard work, good strategies and input from others.[50] Dweck's studies suggest that individuals with a growth mindset put more energy into learning and are likelier to stretch beyond their current capabilities and grow. On the other hand, those with a fixed mindset aren't able to adapt or grow.[51] We all like to think we have a growth mindset regarding ability, but what about the fixed mindset you hold about your identity as a person and as a leader?

Dweck's research found that a pure growth mindset does not exist.[52] We can have a growth mindset about some aspects of ourselves and a fixed mindset about others.[53] And it's been my experience that many people, who are focused on growing in their personal lives, are unaware they are still pinned down by a fixed mindset in their professional lives.

As the storms change and surround us, we don't have to change our identity completely, but we do need to let go of what no longer serves us so that we can develop into the leaders that we need to be. If we're unable to do this, we simply won't be able to find our way into the eye of the storm and centre ourselves.

---

50   Dweck, C. (14 January 2016). 'What Having a "Growth Mindset" Actually Means.' *Harvard Business Review*. https://hbr.org/2016/01/what-having-a-growth-mindset-actually-means.
51   Dweck. What Having a "Growth Mindset" Actually Means.
52   Dweck. What Having a "Growth Mindset" Actually Means.
53   Dweck. What Having a "Growth Mindset" Actually Means.

The curse of assumed knowledge

While our own stories and our fixed inability to move past them can cause us to languish in the storm, they aren't the only things. There's also what I refer to as 'the curse of assumed knowledge'.

On 3 July 1988, during the Iran-Iraq War, an Iranian Airbus A300 was flying over Iran's territorial waters in the Persian Gulf en route from Tehran to Dubai via Bandar Abbas. The USS cruiser Vincennes, a United States Navy guided missile cruiser, was nearby and entered Iranian waters after one of their helicopters drew warning fire from Iranian gunboats operating within Iranian territorial limits. While in Iranian territorial waters, the Vincennes crew came into contact with what they believed to be an F-14 Tomcat jet fighter.

Before this incident, the Vincennes crew had received a briefing that the F-14 Tomcats, which had originally only been configured for combat between aircraft before they were supplied to Iran, had since been reconfigured to enable combat against ground targets. Because of this, the Vincennes crew believed that it was under attack and fired two surface-to-air missiles at the F-14 Tomcat. However, there was no F-14 Tomcat, and the missiles hit an Airbus, killing all 290 people on Iran Air Flight 655.[54]

It is hard to understand exactly what happened. The US military continues to assert the Vincennes crew made multiple attempts to contact the aircraft on military and civilian channels but received no response. The Iranian Government, on the other hand, asserted that the Airbus was transmitting a signal code that clearly identified it as a civilian plane, the Iranian commercial

54   USS Vincennes Shoots Down Iran Air Flight 655. Association for Diplomatic Studies and Training. https://adst.org/2014/07/uss-vincennes-shoots-down-iran-air-flight-655/.

flight was climbing, not diving to attack, and radio messages warning the Airbus were not broadcast on civilian air traffic control frequencies.[55]

If the Iranian aircrew did hear the warnings, it wasn't clear they were meant for them. The US crew expected to encounter military aircraft because they were in active conflict with Iranian gunboats in Iranian waters. Though the Pentagon issued a finding that the Vincennes crew acted appropriately, the situation was full of ambiguity and assumed knowledge, and led to a horrific loss of life.[56]

Of course, that is a highly dramatic life-and-death situation, but assumed knowledge can impact us every day in a myriad of negative ways. Imagine you find a note on your desk. It says, 'Meet me at the park.' It's unclear. The note doesn't say which park, who wrote it or when to meet. Anyone could have written the note, so you don't know what it really means. There are many parks and times you could pick. Ambiguity is like the lost pieces in a puzzle; you know some things but not enough to get a clear picture of the whole thing.

The information available to the people making decisions about whether to fire on the aircraft in Iranian waters was understood differently. There was confusion about how to interpret the facts. When pieces of the puzzle are missing, the evidence tells us that as humans we tend to subconsciously resolve anomalies to fill in the gaps based on what we already know (sometimes called 'top down processing').[57] Because the crew of the Vincennes had already been under fire, they assumed they were at continued risk and interpreted the available information through that lens.

---

55   USS Vincennes Shoots Down Iran Air Flight 655.
56   USS Vincennes Shoots Down Iran Air Flight 655.
57   Cherry, K. (23 August 2023). 'What Is Top-Down Processing?' Verywell Mind. https://www.verywellmind.com/what-is-top-down-processing-2795975#:~:text=Top%2Ddown%20processing%20involves%20perceiving,to%20interpret%20new%20sensory%20information..

Psychologist Arie Kruglanski describes this concept as our need for closure.[58] His studies found that this urge to settle discrepancies and make decisions allows us to get things done and function in the world. It's not a static state. The need for closure varies depending on the context and predisposition of the people involved. However, it is contagious and exacerbated when we're under stress. Tiredness, distracting noises, time pressures and challenges can all increase our desire to make sense of what we're experiencing despite obvious anomalies. We're also more likely to place greater trust in those we know and pay less attention to those we don't.

The crew of the USS cruiser Vincennes learnt this lesson the hard way.

This natural desire for the familiar is called the mere exposure effect.[59] This is a type of cognitive bias in which people like things they already know more about. When we are repeatedly exposed to a stimulus, this increases our familiarity and our liking of it, even if we're unaware of it.

But when one person gets the wrong end of the stick – by identifying a gap and filling it with assumed knowledge or something they're more familiar with – the effect can be contagious and highly detrimental. We get into dangerous territory when we automatically make decisions and move to action because either we feel we are right, or we blindly trust that someone else is. And we're not usually in a situation where we can recognise that we're wrong. In fact, it's been my experience that being wrong often feels the same as being right. It's not until <u>after</u> we realise our decision was based on incorrect information and that we've done the wrong thing that we get that sick feeling in our stomachs

---

58   Krugalanski, A & Webster, D. (1996). 'Motivated Closing of the Mind: "Seizing" and "Freezing". *Psychological Review.* American Psychological Association, Inc. https://www2.psych.ubc.ca/~schaller/Psyc590Readings/Kruglanski1996.pdf.

59   Nickerson, C. (10 October 2023). 'Mere Exposure Effect in Psychology: Biases & Heuristics.' Simply Psychology. https://www.simplypsychology.org/mere-exposure-effect.html.

that signals our mistake (if only we could get that as a pre-mistake warning system!).

When I worked as an executive, I was assigned a new role where I had to learn the ropes. After a period of time, I was asked to approve a variation to purchasing arrangements for a service that was delivered by an external organisation.

Despite the involvement of many people, it was ultimately my decision and my signature on the official record.

The approval documentation was submitted by a highly knowledgeable team with many years of experience in their role. They relied upon official guiding documents that used examples. Unfortunately, those examples were not specifically applicable to this type of approval, and it was later found the team were mistaken in how they interpreted these documents. The guiding document they used didn't include the nuanced information that would have enabled them to provide correct advice.

The document submitted for approval was one of a multitude of documents I had to review and approve with multiple teams each providing advice. There was time pressure, and decisions were based on changing direction to provide the required support and save millions of dollars of taxpayer money.

The documentation was also reviewed by a dedicated finance team before I made the decision to sign on the dotted line. I also assumed, as did the rest of the individuals involved in the process, that the finance team would pick up on any finance-related issues. However, it was later found that they only looked at whether funding was available, not whether the proposal met the broader financial approval requirements. As a result, many people, including me, were involved in a long, disruptive workplace investigation that unearthed how ambiguity was embedded in corporate decision-making processes.

When a staff member told me they had discovered the anomaly, I immediately experienced that sick feeling I always get when I discover I got something I assumed to be right, wrong. I felt sick to the pit of my stomach because, although the decision was made for good and justifiable reasons, it was technically wrong. If you hold a financial delegation, I'm sure you can relate to the potential consequences.

This was a challenging time for me and the entire team. But it was also a growth experience. I learned firsthand the curse of assumed knowledge. Making these types of mistakes is very human and it happens more frequently than most of us would like to admit.

In the time since, I've spent a great deal of time thinking about the series of mistakes – and what led to this ambiguity. While I'm certainly embarrassed to have made the mistake, several colleagues have since told me how easily it could have been them.

This story demonstrates the very human need for closure and the fact that when we feel right, we can unconsciously delete, deny or fail to explore other information that does not support our expectations and feelings. In 1949, Harvard psychologists Jerome Bruner and Leo Postman published a research study in which participants were briefly shown a set of trick playing cards.[60] They were trick cards because some of the card colours were reversed, i.e., some red cards were black and some of the black cards were red.

However, when questioned after briefly seeing the cards, 96% of the study participants described the trick cards they'd glimpsed as normal. Bruner and Postman concluded that people denied the anomalies and saw what they expected to see. People's preconceptions distorted their experience, and their minds filled in the gaps.[61]

---

60   Bruner, J & Postman, L. (1949). 'On the perception of incongruity: a paradigm.' *Journal of Personality*. https://psycnet.apa.org/record/1951-02802-001.

61   Bruner. On the perception of incongruity.

This is not only an issue with what we see or read. We can also get tripped up if there is dissonance between what we are seeing and hearing. This dissonance is called the McGurk effect ('a categorical change in auditory perception induced by incongruent visual speech, resulting in a single perception of hearing something different than what the voice is saying')[62], and it's why it's sometimes a good idea to close our eyes and concentrate on what we're hearing.

The McGurk effect happens when we pay attention to what we see instead of what we hear as we integrate visual and auditory cues. Even professors who have studied the McGurk effect for many years can still get caught out despite being aware of the auditory illusion. You can Google it if you want to experience it yourself.

So, what can we do to avoid ignoring crucial anomalies before making an important decision?

Jamie Holmes, the author of the book *Nonsense: The Power of Not Knowing*, says 'to string decisions that involve ambiguity over a period of days and revisit them in different moods'.[63] This allows you to consider the decision you're making from different perspectives and mindsets, which can help you to better identify where you might be experiencing something erroneously or filling in the gaps.

Unfortunately, that's not always possible when you're in a time-pressured situation. And our inability to do so might keep us in the ravages of the storm.

---

62 Eggermont, J. (2017). *Hearing Loss: Causes, Prevention, and Treatment*. Academic Press.
63 Holmes, J. (2015). *Nonsense: The Power of Not Knowing*. Crown Publishing Group.

It's not as black and white as you think

In recent years we've again seen the rise of polarised thinking and its impact within our communities and different groups within society. War and conflict on the world stage tend to drive black and white thinking. Unfortunately, this leads to claims that one side is purely good, and the other side is evil. And sadly, some people try to explain away atrocities by claiming that the end justifies the means in ridding the world of the 'evil'.

These scenarios are rich fodder for authors and film directors who know that war and conflict is never black and white. There are complexities that exist in the grey space between the leaders and the decisions they make. Complexities that are driven by human empathy or lack thereof, by people's unquestioning sense of righteousness and by people blindly following orders or limiting how they think or act within a narrow range of perceived options.

Numerous films have invited us to explore these complexities, including *Oppenheimer*, winner of the 2024 Academy Award for Best Picture. In the early 1940s, J. Robert Oppenheimer, a brilliant physicist, found himself at the helm of a complex and morally ambiguous scientific initiative: the Manhattan Project. The Manhattan Project was established to develop the world's first nuclear weapons during a time when the Nazi war machine and Allied Forces were in a race to develop new technologies that would give them the winning edge.

The film presents Oppenheimer as a man who is conflicted. Aware of the horrors that would be inflicted by an atomic bomb, he is at the same time aware of the horror that would be unleashed if the Nazis beat the Allies in the more immediate race to win the war.

Some might say that in the early days of the Manhattan Project, Oppenheimer's thinking was black and white about the need to develop the bomb. He is faced with the ethical dilemma of creating a weapon of mass destruction, but he chooses to do so to prevent what he sees as a greater evil.

However, as the project neared completion and the likelihood of Nazi Germany developing its own atomic bomb waned, Oppenheimer's perspective began to shift. It moved from black and white to shades of grey as he began to face the reality that now that the technology behind the bomb was developed, decisions about how it would be used were completely out of his hands. Scientific insights about the bomb's catastrophic potential, coupled with the impending victory of the Allies, led Oppenheimer to advocate for control over nuclear weapons and to oppose their further development and use.

Oppenheimer's thinking evolved in response to changing circumstances and acquiring new knowledge. His journey from the fervent pursuit of the atomic bomb to becoming a proponent of nuclear disarmament underscores the inherent complexities and moral ambiguities that leaders face in systems fraught with uncertainty and rapid change.

His story shows how decisions, viewed in isolation, may seem black or white but reveal a spectrum of greys when viewed within the broader tapestry of context, intention and consequence. It also shows the importance of leadership choices in complex systems and the value of ongoing ethical reflection, even (or especially) when confronted with the most pressing difficulties. Oppenheimer's legacy reveals the complicated nature of leadership and the need to constantly balance action and restraint, power and responsibility.

Now take a moment to reflect on what other people hear you say. Do you frequently skip between extremes, making statements like 'I always' and

'I never', or 'It's perfect' and 'It's impossible'? Do you identify concepts as either purely good or bad?

If so, you're at risk of falling into the trap of black-and-white thinking.

The American Psychological Association calls this dichotomous or 'polarised' thinking because it prevents us from seeing the world as it often is, which is complex, nuanced and full of the shades of grey.[64] Black and white thinking makes surviving complexity and ambiguity harder than it needs to be and stops you from thriving. Yet, it continues to be something that we, as both humans and leaders, face daily.

One reason for polarised thinking is our previous experience of trauma. Researchers such as Marsha Linehan, Judith Herman, Aaron Beck and Bessel van der Kolk believe that when we experience trauma, black-and-white or dichotomous thinking patterns could develop as a coping strategy or to protect us from future harm.

This is why understanding why we think and behave the way we do is essential for every leader. However, if your thinking is impacted by a previous traumatic experience and is anchoring you to your past, I encourage you to seek support from an appropriate professional.

Failing to address black-and-white thinking will restrict your field of vision and you will be blind to the opportunities and insights that can be found between those extreme perspectives. Opportunities and insights that enable you to find your way between the eyes of storms as a centred leader.

---

64   Stanborough, R. (14 January 2020). 'How Black and White Thinking Hurts You (and What You Can Do to Change It.' healthline. https://www.healthline.com/health/mental-health/black-and-white-thinking.

Understanding your reactions

Another thing that holds us back from continually moving into the eye of the storm as leaders is our reactive tendencies. For example, as humans, one reactive tendency that many of us will exhibit is the drive not to lose. I don't say 'the drive to win' on purpose, because, in fact, our brains are wired to prioritise *not losing* over potential gains.[65]

This tendency, known as loss aversion, makes us more sensitive to potential losses than to equivalent gains. In fact, some experts believe that the pain of 'losing' is psychologically twice as powerful as the pleasure of gaining.[66] This particular reactive tendency may see us making leadership decisions that aren't based on proper data and facts but are instead based around this fear of losing.

In the same way, any reactive tendency that is not sufficiently managed can insinuate itself into our leadership and significantly impact our decision-making, team dynamics and overall organisational culture. When you are unaware of those tendencies it can be like you and everyone around you is living with an unseen storm.

Casting shadows

Reactive tendencies are automatic, often subconscious, responses to a situation or stimulus. Our tendencies are shaped by past experiences, habits or emotional triggers and may not align with our values, our beliefs, how we think logically or how we want to act. Being reactive can limit our ability to make thoughtful decisions and influence how we adapt.

---

65   Pilat, D & Krastev, S. 'Loss-aversion, explained.' The Decision Lab. https://thedecisionlab.com/biases/loss-aversion.

66   Pilat. Loss-aversion, explained.

Imagine in the context in which you find yourself there is a light source (a source of truth), and you, as the leader, are the object blocking the light and casting a shadow on everyone and everything around you. The shape and size of that shadow varies depending on your ability to notice what is going on, your ability to manage your response, the intensity of the context and your ability to get sufficient distance. When you get distance from what is happening you can be objective rather than subject to what is happening. But if you cast too large of a shadow, you and your organisation simply can't see the thrust of the situation. And that means you can't move out of the storm to the next eye.

However, reactive tendencies are also a necessary part of being an effective leader. A leader who casts no shadow is inert. They are stuck. They essentially have no impact.

It is rare for a leader to be shadowless. But having too big of a shadow isn't great either. Instead, effective leaders must learn to recognise and harness their reactive tendencies, then use them consciously and strategically. For example:

- Drive will help you get something important done on time.
- Perfectionism ensures critical details are not missed.
- Complying helps you understand and meet expectations.
- Pleasing means you're more likely to listen to people and try to bring them with you.

These tendencies are all essential parts of the shadow we cast as leaders. But we can't allow them to overwhelm other people and situations.

Finding self-awareness

You may be highly educated and have learned models and techniques for leadership, but you need more than trained logic to lead effectively.

A 2020 article in the Journal of Applied Leadership and Management evaluated research findings about the importance of self-awareness for leaders and found a connection between self-awareness and leadership effectiveness.[67] Researchers discussed how modern business interactions require emotional intelligence. But even though emotional intelligence has a critical role in leadership, self-awareness remains largely unexplored.[68]

Interestingly other studies have compared the performance of thousands of CEOs and found the performance of those with an MBA (so, highly trained) was significantly worse than those without (less trained) over a seven-year period.[69] While that doesn't mean that MBAs are not valuable, what it does perhaps show is that training without self-reflection might put you in a worse position as a leader. On the other hand, those with self-awareness are in a better position.[70] It also shows that leadership success celebrated on the covers of business magazines can be fleeting and consistency requires reflection.

Rasmus Hougaard, the founder and CEO of Potential Project, a global leadership development and research firm, conducted a survey of over 1,000 leaders from more than 800 companies in over 100 countries.[71] He and his

---

67   Peter, H. (2020). 'The impact of self-awareness on leadership behavior.' *Journal of Applied Leadership and Management.* https://www.econstor.eu/ bitstream/10419/251923/1/174826270X.pdf.

68   Peter. The impact of self-awareness on leadership behavior.

69   Hougaard, R, Cater, J & Afton, M. (12 January 2018). 'Self-Awareness Can Help Leaders More Than an MBA Can.' *Harvard Business Review.* https://hbr.org/2018/01/self-awareness-can-help-leaders-more-than-an-mba-can.

70   Hougaard. Self-Awareness Can Help Leaders More Than an MBA Can.

71   Hougaard. Self-Awareness Can Help Leaders More Than an MBA Can.

colleagues discovered that leaders at the highest levels tend to be more self-aware than leaders lower in the hierarchy, suggesting that despite our level of formal education we need to improve our self-awareness as our leadership responsibility grows.[72]

Self-awareness can be the difference between being pushed along by unseen forces or noticing the weather patterns and choosing what course to take.

Leaders who are self-aware can make the shift from playing not to lose to intentionally moving towards what they want to achieve with vision and purpose.

However, it's sometimes easier said than done.

---

72   Hougaard. Self-Awareness Can Help Leaders More Than an MBA Can.

CHAPTER 3

What Else Needs Letting Go

When I first met my partner, he was petrified of dentists – not just one, but all of them. This stems from an accident he had when he was a child that led to him needing dental work, and his terrible experience left a deep mark. He avoided any dentist for years until he knew he couldn't put it off any longer.

At the time, I had been seeing my dentist since I was three years old. Going to see Dr O'Connor was like going to visit an old family friend. I shared my partner's deep fear with him, and he said, 'If you can get him here, I'll do the rest.'

It took some doing because my partner's fear of seeing a dentist felt worse than his dental pain. But eventually, my partner agreed to give Dr O'Connor a chance.

That first time was a blinding success, and he agreed to go back and start a long series of treatments. I was amazed each time my partner came home and raved about the wonderful Dr O'Connor and his dental assistants despite all the needles, drills and discomfort.

I share this story because, at some point, most people find themselves more afraid of the experience they imagine could occur than the experience itself. We create vivid mind pictures of the horrible experience we anticipate. The imagined experience and the feelings it generates make us uncomfortable, so we avoid putting ourselves in that situation. Yet, how many times, when we finally feel the fear and do it anyway, do we look back and wonder why we waited so long?

It's like standing in front of a closed door in someone else's house during a blackout at night. The feelings about what could be behind the door are intense but, once we open it, we usually find ourselves in just another room.

To be centred leaders, we'll have to learn how to manage these fears.

Trying to control the uncontrollable

Think back to a time when your scope of responsibility expanded and the pressure to perform mounted. How did you respond? Did you loosen the reigns, or hold on tighter? If it's the second, then you might have been trying to control the uncontrollable.

Trying to control the uncontrollable can manifest in many ways.

I once agreed to take responsibility for part of a direct report's portfolio because I was extremely worried about this person burning out. It seemed like the responsible thing to do but, in hindsight, the person was inadvertently disempowered, and their confidence was damaged.

My attempt to control the uncontrollable resulted in perverse consequences and taught me an important lesson about leadership. Trying to control everything can stifle creativity, hinder the emergence of better options and, ultimately, damage the team. It's like keeping a baby bird safe in its nest but then realising too late that you've stopped it from learning to fly.

In a 2020 podcast episode about anxiety, calm and over-/under-functioning, University of Houston research professor Brené Brown said that people who over-function tend to step in, take control and become hyper-rational when they're anxious.[73] Instead of stepping back, giving up control and becoming less competent under stress they amp it up a level and do even more to try and ensure success.[74]

As difficult as it may be, letting go and trusting your team is essential. Instead of trying to control everything, you need to loosen up. Yes, I know, it's easier to say than do when there's a lot at stake. But it's worth it! It's not about letting your team sink or swim. It's about setting clear parameters that provide the rigour needed to achieve deliverables while, at the same time, giving your team the space to experiment, try new things and take ownership.

The good news is there's a positive correlation between team members who perceive a strong link between their actions, expected goals and outcomes, and delegated tasks being performed successfully. Those are the team members who believe they are the masters of their own fate. They tend to be more confident, alert, and directive in attempting to influence their external environment as well.

---

73   Brown, B. (3 April 2020). 'Brené Brown on Anxiety, Calm, and Over-/Under-Functioning.' [Audio podcast]. Brené Brown. https://brenebrown.com/podcast/brene-on-anxiety-calm-over-under-functioning/.

74   Brown. Brené Brown on Anxiety, Calm, and Over-/Under-Functioning.

If you find that you're a leader who struggles with trying to control the uncontrollable, the solution is to use self-reflection to identify where you're struggling to let go of control and the consequences – current and future. If you aren't able to do this, you'll be stuck in the storm and never truly find the eye.

If you want a team who externalises and is totally dependent on you to get anything done, then by all means hold those reigns as tight as you can. You'll end up with a nest of birds unable to fly alone while others leave the nest as soon as possible.

Perfectionism – a two-sided coin

Being a perfectionist can both help and hinder a leader striving to be more centred. Another way we refer to this (as Brené Brown did in her podcast) is 'over-functioning'.

If you haven't figured it out yet, one of my personal challenges is over-functioning.

When I was a very junior member of staff, I found myself in a situation where I was expected to assure a chief executive officer that he had every hard copy approval for every new position created over the last twenty years. However, I knew the hard copy filing system was less than accurate. The Chief Executive would call me daily seeking assurances. It got to the point where I would start physically shaking every time the phone rang because as much as I wanted to, and despite how hard I worked, I could not give him the assurance he wanted and know that I was being truthful.

This was a catalyst for me initially seeking professional help for my tendency towards perfectionism. For years after that I thought I had a handle on it. I could use it when needed but also back off when it mattered.

However, in 2013 when I was honoured to be awarded a scholarship to attend the Women's Leadership Forum at Harvard Business School, I learned that perfectionism could manifest in many ways.

At the forum we would meet each day with our own 'board of advisers' – a small group facilitated by a professional coach. Our advisers' role was to help us identify our strengths and weaknesses, articulate and overcome our personal leadership challenges and develop an action plan focused on our personal leadership approach so we could continue developing as leaders long after the program.

Towards the end of the week, we were expected to take turns presenting to our fellow advisers and the coach. Each night I would go back to my room and keep working on my presentation. Whenever we were asked who's next, I would beg off saying 'I'm not ready yet'. Then I would keep working on it.

The penny finally dropped when there was no more time, and I had no choice but to present. The irony was that instead of helping me focus on how I could build on my existing strengths, my anxiety and imposter feelings about whether I deserved to be participating in a Harvard University course had pushed my perfectionist tendencies into overdrive.

To get there, I had jumped through twice the number of hoops as the other participants. However, I still didn't feel that I was good enough.

What drives perfectionism is different for everyone who lives with it. It's like a chameleon, morphing and changing as your context changes, your values are challenged or your insecurities are triggered. Personally, I equate it to an addiction. It's not something you're ever free of. It's why I refer to myself as

a 'recovering perfectionist' and always try to remember what Voltaire said –
'The perfect is the enemy of the good.'

If you're not a perfectionist, I'm sure you've experienced the impact of the positive and negative sides of perfectionism in others.

It's not all bad. There are pros and cons when it comes to perfectionism.

Pros	Cons
Keen eye for detail and meticulous work	Losing sight of the big picture
High standards and striving for excellence	Inflexibility and unwillingness to share until something is just right
Persistence and drive to find solutions	Fear of failure and risk aversion
Systematic and thorough approach	Overthinking, procrastination and delayed action

There is a time and place for tapping into our tendencies. One on my friends is a highly-skilled technician who works on multi-million-dollar machinery. In some contexts, his tendency to want to check everything five times could be annoying. However, in a context where a loose screw could cause tens of thousands of dollars of damage he is revered for the quality and reliability of this work.

So while perfectionism isn't all bad, the key for leaders who have this trait is knowing how to use those tendencies to best effect. Giving free reign to perfectionist tendencies can be like a hiker on a mountain trail who is constantly checking and adjusting their backpack, making sure that everything is in its place, and the weight distribution is perfectly balanced. While this attention to detail and preparedness may be helpful, it can also slow the hiker down and cause them to lose sight of the trail ahead. The hiker may become so fixated on perfecting the details of their backpack that they forget to enjoy the scenery and may even miss important trail markers or overlook potential hazards on the path.

Similarly, a leader who is a perfectionist must be continually centring themselves or they may become so focused on perfecting the details of a problem or situation that they lose sight of the big picture and miss important opportunities or solutions.

It is essential to balance the benefits of perfectionism with the need to stay flexible and adaptable if you want to become and remain a centred leader.[75]

Be aware of when perfectionism is becoming, as Brené Brown says, 'a self-destructive and addictive belief system that fuels this primary thought: If I look perfect, and do everything perfectly, I can avoid or minimize the painful feelings of shame, judgment, and blame.'[76]

When our own standards get in the way

One client who led a function within an organisation had extremely high standards. Their chief executive loved that they could always deliver on the vision and exceeded expectations. However, the work area reporting through that senior executive experienced significant turnover and tension as members of the team either left because they couldn't sustain meeting that

---

75   Stoeber, J., & Otto, K. (2006). 'Positive conceptions of perfectionism: Approaches, evidence, challenges.' *Personality and Social Psychology Review.* https://pubmed.ncbi.nlm.nih.gov/17201590/.

76   Brown, B. The Gifts of Imperfection. (2020). Vermilion – Mass Market.

constant high standard or tried to fight against the standard, often losing out to the person who had the greater organisational power.

Unfortunately, when we hold ourselves or others to rigid, uncompromising standards in complex situations, we can miss important nuances or fail to consider alternative perspectives, and this can result in ineffective decision-making or unintended consequences.

In complex situations (converging storms!), it's important to recognise that multiple perspectives or approaches can be valid. Even if options don't meet our initial high standards, we need to keep an open mind and listen without judgement to different perspectives before discounting them. It also requires an ability to tolerate some level of risk and experimentation to avoid stifling creativity, innovation and learning.

However, it doesn't mean we should throw our standards out the window. Setting a clear expectation of excellence and quality can inspire and motivate people to do their best work and enable them to work towards the best possible outcome.

Standards based on our values can also help us prioritise effort and make difficult decisions about what does and does not get done. Our values provide a frame of reference for evaluating options and weighing trade-offs to determine the best course of action. Holding to standards aligned to our values also helps us build trust and credibility with others because our colleagues, customers and stakeholders know what they can consistently expect.

However, the risk with continually holding to high standards is that we hold to a single 'right' answer. Deliberately introducing disruptive elements or perspectives can reduce this risk and encourage more experimentation and creativity.

Just as a blindfold limits our ability to see and navigate our environment, high standards can sometimes limit our ability to see and navigate the complexities of a situation. Loosening our grip on high standards by asking 'Does it matter?', and 'Will it enable what is needed next?', can provide insights about the need to adapt or set completely new standards so you can navigate change and complexity more effectively.

The 1970 Apollo 13 space mission is a good example of the criticality of adjusting standards to suit the situation. When that mission experienced a crippling explosion that compromised the air filtration system, the astronauts aboard faced a dire situation – a lethal buildup of carbon dioxide threatened their lives. Back at NASA's Mission Control, the team of engineers, scientists and technicians faced an unprecedented challenge. They had to devise a solution using only the materials available on the spacecraft.[77]

They cobbled together a makeshift filtration system using unexpected materials, including a cover from a flight manual. This ad-hoc solution was far from perfect; it wouldn't have passed pre-launch standards. However, it was precisely what was needed for the situation. The team quickly communicated the design to the astronauts, who, despite being cognitively impaired due to the rising carbon dioxide levels, successfully replicated the filter.

In life-threatening circumstances, the NASA team had to let go of their usual high standards and focus on what was necessary to save the astronauts' lives. Their ability to adapt and prioritise a 'good enough' solution over a perfect one resolved the immediate crisis but also shows it is possible to maintain a standard of excellence and remain open to unconventional, practical solutions.

---

77   Briand, V. (21 April 2020). 'Apollo 13: five crisis management lessons from a successful failure.' *Medium.* https://medium.com/@virginiebriand/apollo-13-five-crisis-management-lessons-from-a-successful-failure-1202da0cc744.

Obviously, this was a life-threatening situation, but the principle of letting go and adapting in response to the needs of the situation also holds true in an organisational context.

Steve Jobs, also known for his high standards, recognised the importance of being adaptable and willing to change course when necessary, especially in complex situations where the 'right' answer may not always be clear.

When you blindly cling to standards, you inadvertently push yourself towards being wrong. However, when you're aware of this tendency you can take your cue from Steve Jobs who said, 'I have no problem with being wrong, I just don't like being wrong for very long.'

Held back by toxic resilience

As we develop as leaders, we gain a sense of who and how we should be. We often respond to the expectations of more senior experienced leaders and the cultures of the organisations we work in. Some of the expectations I picked up were the importance of being optimistic and inspiring confidence in my team, maintaining or improving morale, and being a good corporate citizen or toeing the line once a decision has been made.

This approach may have served at different times in my career but when the perfect storms were raging, it was less than helpful.

I ended up putting enormous pressure on myself to stay positive in even the most unreasonable circumstances. If I was in front of our team, I could usually be seen with a smile on my face, always on the lookout for a silver lining. But as I let the need to be positive take priority, I began to stop noticing my own emotional signals. My reactive tendencies began to amplify but not consistently.

I would keep myself tightly under control when the next major or important challenge emerged in the course of my official duties. However, I would completely over-react at minor things, because in the moment they felt enormous.

I remember letting my self-righteousness take over when someone, who was going through their own moment, parked in my work-assigned parking space. The car park was full, so I had to exit and find parking at my own expense. I got stuck in a 20-minute one-way traffic loop that made me late for an important meeting.

I was so incensed I felt the need to share with the other person what they had done to me. The note I wrote was factual, it wasn't abusive, but it was not my finest moment. I failed to think about what the other person was going through. I assumed I was right, and they were in the wrong. I stopped looking at the bigger picture and only focused on what it meant for me.

Over the years I had learned how to show up in front of the team. Being optimistic was a learned behaviour. Unfortunately, as the context around me changed, and the perfect storms continued to rage, I was unaware that my optimism had shifted to toxic resilience.

Recognising toxic resilience

Toxic resilience happens when you persistently maintain unhealthy behaviours, attitudes or relationships, fuelled by a misguided sense of resilience. Instead of enabling your growth and well-being, this form of resilience anchors you in a harmful pattern.

Typically, it arises when your ability to withstand adversity, a trait usually deemed positive, is misdirected towards sustaining destructive environments or relationships. For example, you're in a damaging work situation and you pride yourself on your capacity to endure over every other consideration. [78]

Being optimistic is not a bad thing. But like all strengths it can become a weakness when you let it shift into overdrive, when it starts casting a bigger shadow than is healthy for you and those around you. That's when it can become a learned behaviour, something we can do well, have probably used too much or we know we need to do to keep ourselves out of trouble or meet expectations. However, if overused they can turn into weaknesses, deplete your energy and reduce your resilience.[79]

Getting stuck in quicksand

At a packed event for Fostering Executive Women Alumni at the Queensland University of Technology, Dame Quentin Bryce shared insights that resonated with many aspiring leaders in the audience. Known for her wisdom and experience, Dame Quentin offered a refreshing perspective on decision-making and career progression.

Dame Quentin's key advice was simple yet profound: say yes when opportunity knocks. She emphasised the importance of not getting bogged down by doubts about readiness or skill levels. Instead of succumbing to analysis paralysis, she advocated for trusting one's instincts and having the confidence to leap into new opportunities.

She encouraged us to avoid getting stuck worrying about whether we were ready or knew everything we needed to know. Her advice was to believe in

---

78   Grant, A. (April 2019). When strength becomes weakness. [Video]. Ted Conferences. https://www.ted.com/talks/worklife_with_adam_grant_when_strength_becomes_ weakness/transcript?subtitle=en.

79   Kaplan, R & Kaiser, R. (February 2009). 'Stop Overdoing Your Strengths.' *Harvard Business Review*. https://hbr.org/2009/02/stop-overdoing-your-strengths.

ourselves and decide whether we had the support we needed to work out how to make the situation work after we took the leap.

In essence, she told us not to miss opportunities because we're stuck in the quicksand of analysis paralysis. In other words, we get caught in a never-ending loop where we're trying to exclude all the hints or clues that tell us that what we know might be wrong or that what we want to do may not work. It's made worse when we feel we have too many choices and fear choosing the wrong one. We just don't know which information will help us make a decision, and so our decision-making is frozen. And this means we can miss what's happening in the bigger picture.

When we get stuck in the quicksand, we:

- Stop moving towards what we want or need.
- Miss opportunities.
- See increased business costs or lost income or revenue.
- Waste time (and permit our team to waste time) that could be spent doing something more productive.
- Create the opportunity for lost confidence with people upstream and downstream.
- Tend to obsess about the wrong issue and miss important clues that action is required elsewhere.

Cognitive and behavioural scientists Amos Tversky and Eldar Shafir found that the presence of conflicting information increases our tendency to defer decisions or stick with default options.[80] They found the more time people had, the more likely they were to delay action and stay on the more familiar or safe road.[81] Unfortunately, these phenomena keep us stuck in the quicksand.

---

80   Tversky, A & Shafir, E. (November 1992). 'Choice under Conflict: The Dynamics of Deferred Decision.' *Psychological Science*. https://www.jstor.org/stable/40062808.

81   Tversky. Choice under Conflict.

If Dame Quentin had focused on all the reasons why she couldn't be the first woman to do something or spent a long time weighing up the options when opportunities presented, she almost certainly wouldn't have been Australia's first female Governor-General. Her success was not about knowing everything in advance but about being willing to take the plunge and figure things out along the way.

In their book *Big Feelings: How to Be Okay When Things Are Not Okay*, Liz Fosslien and Mollie West Duffy explain, 'Your plans and answers don't need to be highly detailed, so avoid getting swept up in analysis paralysis. The goal is just to build your confidence in the idea that you would be able to handle the situation.' This sounds like what Dame Quentin attributed to her success.

It's unlikely Dame Quentin blindly jumped into opportunities, and far more likely she used her curiosity to overcome the problems of:

- Being captured by initial beliefs like 'I can't do it', 'I'm not ready' or 'I don't have the skills'.
- Failing to test those beliefs.
- Explaining away data that is inconsistent with those beliefs.

We can face this challenge at any time, not only when faced with a career opportunity, but we have to face it if we want to move into the eye of the storm and more centred leadership.

Conclusion

In the last two chapters we've spent a lot of time focusing on the factors that can hold you back from becoming a centred leader. These could be the traps of past successes, complacency or even overconfidence. We must move past these various hindrances, whether personal or professional, to avoid them taking on deeper meaning, shaping our identity and skewing our decision-making. Most importantly, they keep us in the complexity of the storm when left unaddressed, causing us to cling to familiar (and ultimately unsuccessful) leadership methods despite changing circumstances.

To become centred leaders, we have to learn how to navigate between the eyes of the storms, letting go of our self-imposed limitations and learning to adapt so we can weather the inevitable challenges.

We can't stop the storm, but we can move to safety – to the eye of the storm – and determine the next right steps. And we do that by using the Centring Star as our guide.

GETTING CENTRED

CHAPTER 4

Centred in the Storm

If you've been feeling swamped by the obstacles preventing you from achieving leadership excellence, there's a lot of hope. This is where you move away from what is getting in the way of being a centred leader and focus on how you can become that leader. And it involves getting centred in the storm.

Getting centred in the storm

Getting centred in the storm begins with getting centred in yourself. Authentic leadership has risen in popularity since the early 2000s. Being an authentic leader means using your values, beliefs, and principles as an inner compass that guides your decision-making, acting with integrity and taking responsibility for your actions. In its simplest form, many people think of it as being true to yourself.

So, how do you stay true to yourself when the pressure from so many external forces means you start playing not to lose instead of moving towards who you need to be next?

You start by remembering that a centred leader is not their context. Instead, they effectively manage themselves in the context.

Centred leaders don't let the forces surrounding them sweep away who they are at their core. They respond to their context with adaptive authenticity because they can be themselves with more skill.

During an April 2023 McKinsey and Company podcast, Harvard Business School professor and former CEO of Medtronic Bill George said, 'Many people want everyone else to change, but they also have to adapt. With all the crises we have, one of the keys to being an authentic leader is being adaptable to constant change.'[82]

I didn't know who I wanted to be as a little girl. I loved dressing up in the clothes I would find in both my parents' wardrobes. Some days I was my mother in a cast-off ball gown; other days I was my father dressed up to go to work. I playfully explored those different personas, and I'm neither of those people today.

My children had their own dress-up box that we kept in the cupboard under the stairs. One day my son was a firefighter; the next, he would be a policeman. Sometimes he would try my daughter's mermaid tail on for fun, but he kept going back to his Power Ranger's onesie until it split up the backside giving everyone an unexpected view. It eventually wore out, and he had to discard

---

82   Dewar, C. (5 April 2023). Leading with authenticity: A conversation with Bill George [Podcast transcript]. *McKinsey & Company*. https://www.mckinsey.com/capabilities/ strategy-and-corporate-finance/our-insights/leading-with-authenticity-a-conversation- with-bill-george.

it. He didn't let it go easily, but after enough people told him it was well past time, he came to the same realisation.

Finding and being your authentic leadership self is no different.

In her research, London Business School Professor Herminia Ibarra found that we tend to pull back towards familiar behaviours and leadership styles and protect our self-identity when pushed beyond our comfort zone.[83] This can lead us to grab hold of authenticity as an excuse for sticking with what makes us comfortable.

Ibarra calls the process 'outsight'.[84] It requires plunging yourself into experimenting with different experiences and then reflecting on valuable external perspectives to be more 'adaptively authentic' in the way you lead.

She says, 'Action changes who we are and what we believe is worth doing' and 'the only way we grow as leaders is by stretching the limits of who we are—doing new things that make us uncomfortable but that teach us through direct experience who we want to become'.[85]

Ignoring your need to adapt as a leader is like sticking to a VHS tape while everyone else is streaming their favourite shows. If that sounds like you, get with the times and lead like you're running an on-demand streaming service. Now is the time to recognise different facets of yourself and to develop the confidence to try on new versions as you develop the habits that will help you navigate and not only survive but thrive in the turbulent spaces between the eyes of the storms.

---

83   Ibarra, H. (19 December 2014). 'The authenticity paradox.' *Harvard Business Review.* https://herminiaibarra.com/the-authenticity-paradox/.

84   Ibarra. The authenticity paradox.

85   Ibarra. The authenticity paradox.

How does this work? It starts with knowing your values and strengths and then using the Centring Star to continually guide you to act in alignment with those values. When you know your values, and actively behave in alignment with them, they become your tether as you move through the inevitable storms you will encounter. In other words, your values keep you tethered to the Centring Star.

Imagine you're a navigator of a tall ship, completely dependent on the placement of the sun and stars to find your way from one place to the next or through unknown territory. The Centring Star is your guiding light. It's always there, enduring and guiding you through storm after storm. It sits above and slightly forward of you, enabling you to focus on the next right thing. As you move from one eye of the storm to the next, you'll find yourself moving from the right thing to the next right thing again and again. Over time, you'll learn how to plot a directional path to continually recentre yourself in the eye of the storm, even when it's a perfect storm.

It won't all be roses, though. Sometimes, you need to adapt how you live in alignment with your values – not because they aren't important to you anymore but because they've become unworkable in specific situations.

When you use the points of the Centring Star as your guide, you'll be able to work through these challenges as they arise, develop your intuitive wisdom and learn when you should and shouldn't trust your gut.

Tethered by your values and character strengths

Values are important beliefs and principles that guide our behaviour and decision-making. They act like a compass, helping us decide what is right and wrong for us and how to behave in different situations.

You can think of your values as guardrails on a winding road. They keep you from veering off into dangerous territory and offer you freedom to navigate the path ahead with a sense of security. As you traverse the twists and turns associated with leading through volatility, complexity, ambiguity and uncertainty, your values make sure you don't lose yourself.

Steve Hayes, a Professor of Psychology at the University of Nevada and one of the founders of Acceptance and Commitment Therapy (ACT) defines values as 'intentional qualities that join together a string of moments into a meaningful path.'[86]

These intentional qualities – or values – are deeply personal and can include things like honesty, kindness, fairness, gratitude, freedom, respect and responsibility. Your values are yours – you choose them. No one else should tell you what your personal values are. They may or may not align with those of your organisation. If they don't, you'll need to understand how your beliefs and principles enable you to behave as expected and contribute positively at work.

These beliefs and principles shape our interactions and how we handle challenges and contribute at work, with our family and friends and to our communities. Because when we live in alignment with our values, we create a consistent and trusted way of being that others can rely on and respect.

---

86   Hayes, S & Smith, S. (2005). *Get Out Of Your Mind & Into Your Life: The New Acceptance & Commitment Therapy.* New Harbinger Publications.

In the same way that your values are at the core of who you are as a person, they're also at the core of being an authentic leader. When you lead with your values, you know and show what you believe is important. In other words, you walk the talk. Leading with your values sets you up for sustainable success, especially when it comes to behaving ethically and with integrity.

Along with our values, our core character strengths are the roots that ground us. When we hold to them, we feel authentic and engaged. They enable us to be like a tree with strong roots, knowing when to stand firm and when to adapt, bending with the wind to avoid breaking. Our willingness to learn, adapt and grow towards the light breaking through the storm is what allows us to bend in the wind and thrive amidst adversity and, ultimately, to get and remained centred.

Finding your core values

The first step to getting centred is to be clear about your values and strengths.

In her book *Dare to Lead,* Brené Brown encourages leaders to identify and focus on just two core values that define who they are and what they stand for.[87] She argues this clarity helps leaders make decisions and act with integrity, even in challenging situations.[88]

However, for some people, this can be a little too challenging to do in practice. I find that people can more meaningfully connect with their values if they identify two core values and up to three other supporting values.

For example, a leader guiding their team through a major organisational change might prioritise the value of integrity by being transparent about

---

87   Brown, B. (15 October 2018). *Dare to Lead: Brave Work. Tough Conversations. Whole Hearts.* Vermilion.

88   Brown. Dare to Lead.

the challenges ahead and the value of empathy by actively listening to team members' concerns. Integrity and empathy are this leader's core values. But these core values are supported by the values of courage, accountability and adaptability. Courage enables them to make tough decisions despite the discomfort, accountability ensures that they and their team follow through on commitments and adaptability helps them adjust plans as needed while staying true to their core values.

However, another leader whose core values are creativity and collaboration might encourage their team to brainstorm new ideas and work together to bring those ideas to life. Their supporting values might then be openness, trust and curiosity. The value of openness fosters an environment where all ideas are welcomed. Their value of trust ensures that team members feel safe to share their thoughts without fear of judgement. And their value of curiosity drives their continual search for innovative solutions.

Your values are your own. Their interpretation and application are unique to you. If you find identifying two core values and three supporting values works well for you, remember that their status as either core or supporting values can change depending on your context or lived experience. Those five values are likely to feature in your top five list consistently, but their order may change.

Let's return to the leader who prioritised integrity and empathy as their core values while guiding their team through a major organisational change. Let's assume they're now on the other side of the change and are managing a high-pressure client relationship. They've slightly realigned their five values in response to the situation.

Empathy and courage have come to the fore. They prioritise their value of empathy because they are focused on understanding and addressing the client's needs and concerns. However, they find that courage has become more important than integrity – integrity is still there, but it's dropped down a level. This is because the leader needs to make tough decisions and communicate openly given the difficult repercussions they must manage with their client.

The leader's value of integrity will be crucial for maintaining honesty and trust in interactions with their client. The leader's value of accountability enables them to meet the client's expectations and deliver on their commitments. The leader's value of adaptability allows them to adjust strategies and approaches based on the client's feedback and evolving requirements.

But what if your values don't feel entirely clear to you right now? If this is your situation, I encourage you to commit to completing at least one of these exercises to regain that clarity:

1. Reflective journalling
2. Values card exercise
3. Guided visualisation

Reflective journalling

Spend time writing about significant moments in your life – both positive and challenging. Reflect on what was most important to you during these times, what guided your decisions and how you felt about the outcomes. This reflective practice can help reveal recurring themes that point to your core values. Prompts to help you get started with your journalling might include:

'What was the most fulfilling experience I've had, and why?'

'When have I felt most proud of my actions, and what values were at play?'

You could also chat with a voice-to-text application like Otter.ai if you're more comfortable talking than journalling. You can use its artificial intelligence capabilities to ask it questions about the common themes that arise during the conversation. You can even ask it to suggest a relative prioritisation of your values based on the prevalence of the emerging themes.

Values cards exercise

Value cards are a popular tool for identifying and prioritising values. They typically feature a wide range of values, each represented by a word or short phrase. Each card represents a different value (e.g., honesty, compassion, success).[89] To use the value cards, you first decide on the context, i.e., work, home, relationships etc. Then sort the cards into three piles: very important, important and not important. Then, you narrow the very important pile down to just two core and three supporting values.

Repeat the exercise for different contexts to see whether your values are consistently the same or vary slightly depending on the context. Completing this exercise forces you to prioritise your most important values in context. It will also provide insight into how others can experience you in those different contexts and whether the same people will likely have a consistent experience across those contexts.

Guided visualisation

Another option is seeking support from a mentor or coach to guide you through a visualisation exercise. In a guided visualisation, you will be asked to close your eyes and imagine a scenario in which you are living your ideal life. You'll be encouraged to think about what you're doing, who you're with and what principles guide your actions. Afterwards, your mentor or coach

---

89   If you don't have any values cards handy you can download a free pdf to make your own by going to www.susanneleboutillier.com/centred/resources.

will help you capture the most prominent values in this ideal scenario. This type of guided approach taps into your subconscious preferences and values. As with the value cards, you can also try visualising your ideal life in different contexts.

If you do this with a coach or mentor, they may notice things as an external observer that you're not consciously aware of, and help you clarify your values through curious questioning and deeper conversation. The questions they ask should enable you to explore your beliefs, motivations and past experiences and guide you towards recognising your core and supporting values.

When values become unworkable

Have you ever seen the Facebook posts that start, 'I was this old when…' then go on to share some well-known hack the person was oblivious about until they reached an age well past when they should have known?

I have my own 'I was this old when…' story. Unfortunately, it wasn't a well-known hack and not knowing this thing significantly impacted my wellbeing.

Many people in my professional network are purpose-driven individuals whose core beliefs and values are in some way aligned with making a positive difference and contributing to society. They also work in some of the most complex, challenging environments, where a change in one part of the system, albeit well-intentioned, can lead to a negative, perverse consequence in another part of the system. Enormous effort goes into convincing people who hold the purse strings why they should approve an investment and what they can expect in return, knowing those results cannot be controlled.

Continually probing and sensing the next right thing to do is par for the course.

When I was inside 'the system,' I kept pushing to the next milestone because the actions being taken were aligned with deeply-held core beliefs and values. Those beliefs and values pushed me ever on. For example, my values drove me to find ways to create quality clinical training capacity so a tsunami of new medical graduates could complete their mandatory training requirements, be registered as doctors and be there when my children were adults and had their own children.

Being pushed by my values meant that I was on a never-ending roller coaster ride of achievement highs and incredibly long, hard slogs. And the entire time I was keenly watching for signs about whether the change I was trying to influence was heading in the right or wrong direction and, when I found it was wrong, rapidly adapting, all whilst trying to manage a diverse array of stakeholder expectations.

If you've been there then you know that, when you keep getting to that high point, the number of roller coaster carriages you're pushing up that hill keeps multiplying. But you keep pushing because you think you are doing the right thing. When you finally burn out, the sting in the tail is that you are no longer doing the right thing.

Numerous milestone birthdays passed before I realised that actions grounded in and aligned with my values were not always the best course of action. Not when working in strict alignment with them, no matter what, also meant driving myself into the ground. That didn't serve me or those close to me at home or work.

If you find yourself in this position, you'll also find that when you're under significant, continued pressure without a break you start casting shadows (remember the shadows!). You start losing awareness in the moment and you won't have the capacity to be your best self. Of course, it's difficult to see this in the moment.

If you're in this boat, I invite you to remove those rose-coloured glasses that make you believe it will be okay if you can just get up this next hill. Please put those glasses on the table and stand back. Take a deep breath, ground yourself in the moment, not your values, and look objectively at what is happening.

How big is your shadow?

If it's bigger than it should be, it's time to apply the workability test. I'm forever grateful to the wonderful Dr Rachel Collis for introducing me to this concept during a coaching conversation.

Workability Test

First, ask yourself, 'Are your values workable in this specific context?'

If the answer is no, show yourself the same kindness you would a friend and find a way to step back and loosen your hold on being driven by values-aligned action. Instead, hand the reins over to someone else for a while and take the time to rest, recover and regain your perspective. You may not need to step away from work, but you do need support to get some other perspectives.

Not doing this was one of my big regrets. I felt I was too busy to spend time with my executive coach but that's when I needed their support the most.

When you're ready to step back into the fray, it's time to take the second step. That is to reframe how you look at the situation.

Imagine your values are in a VIP area protected by a velvet rope (again, thank you, Rachel). Before you let anything past that velvet rope, decide if it's worthy of entering your VIP area, given its limited capacity. Choose to invest your values in what's most important in this present moment and let go of what does not serve the here and now.

If you're finding that hard, take some time to think about what Dr Kelly G. Wilson, one of the co-founders of ACT, said:

> 'Learning to sit with ambiguity can be a very important start at a life liberated from anxiety—and the way to do it is to resist the urge to chase answers to questions that may actually be unanswerable.'[90]

Finally, when you've thought about what that means for you – give yourself permission to let go! If you're too deeply enmeshed to do it by yourself, find a trusted companion who can help you ease your way out with grace and integrity.

Finding your strengths

Strengths and values are closely related. Your character strengths are the positive traits reflected in your thoughts, feelings and behaviours, such as kindness, honesty and perseverance. They tend to have the same labels you would expect to find on a value, but they are the inherent qualities you naturally express when you are at your best. They're who you are without effort. On the other hand, your values are principles and beliefs that are applied more consciously to guide your choices and actions. Because they're closely aligned to our values and moral compass, you may find some of your character strengths and values overlap.

---

90   Wilson, K & DuFrene, T. (1 May 2010). *Things Might Go Horribly, Horribly Wrong: A Guide to Life Liberated from Anxiety.* New Harbinger Publications.

If you're unsure which strengths are your character strengths, you may wish to take one of the surveys developed by the VIA Institute on Character.[91] Their research shows that understanding and applying one's character strengths can boost confidence, enable one to strengthen important relationships and reduce stress.

Your character strengths will also be a tether to your core sense of self as you learn new skills and develop the confidence to be who you need to be next in order to navigate the inevitable storms, both the ones you see coming and those you don't. Your general character strengths are not your only strengths. You also possess other 'assessed strengths' which you can identify through assessments like the Cappfinity Strengths Profile[92] or Clifton Strengths Profile[93].

These assessed strengths profiles focus on your abilities in specific contexts, especially professional ones. While your character strengths define who you are and naturally surface when you're at your best, assessed strengths pinpoint specific skills or behaviours that help you perform effectively in work and leadership roles at a point in time. These strengths can energise you or drain you if overused or learned and applied as a protective strategy.

Remember that character strengths anchor your leadership in authenticity and integrity which in turn help you on your centred leadership journey. They remain consistent, providing stability through various experiences. Assessed strengths, however, are situational and evolve as you grow professionally. They serve as practical tools to address specific challenges and achieve your goals. They tend to change, often after you either grow through struggle or overuse an assessed strength to the point where it affects your resilience.

---

91   https://www.viacharacter.org/
92   www.strengbthsprofile.com
93   www.gallup.com/cliftonsrengths/en/home.aspx

Your strengths help keep you centred

It's important to understand your character and assessed strengths to stay centred. Your character strengths ground you in your identity, while your assessed strengths offer clear ways to navigate your leadership role. Together with your values, they act as tethers so you can venture out from the eye of the storm confident in who you are, so you feel safe to forge a path to the next eye of the storm.

When you find it tough to align with your values, show self-compassion and do what you can. Accept that withdrawal or stepping aside might be the right move at times. As author Robin Sharma says, 'Lean into your fears. Go out to your edges. Because the place where your greatest limits live is also the place where your greatest growth lies.'

The Centring Star

By now you should know how to tether your leadership to who you are at your core to stay true to yourself as you navigate the storms. The next crucial step in becoming a centred leader is learning how to operate in alignment with the Centring Star, your guide to navigating through a landscape of rolling storms so that you feel safe to lead in a world that is constantly changing.

The Centring Star

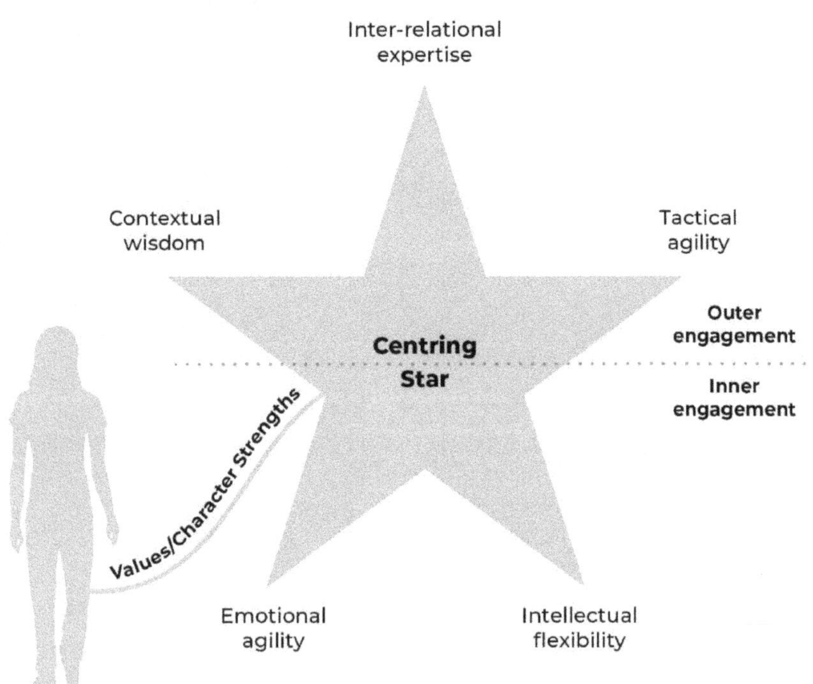

Operating in alignment with the Centring Star

Like the moon, the Centring Star is not fully visible to the casual observer. Two of the five points, emotional agility and intellectual flexibility, are about your internal engagement, and these will only be fully visible to you. The other three points, contextual wisdom, inter-relational expertise and tactical agility, are about how you engage with the world external to you, and these may be visible to those around you.

The star is imbued with wisdom. Personal wisdom about your identity and reactive tendencies, social wisdom about interacting with other people and organisations and contextual wisdom which enables you to get deeply centred in the now and make sense of what is happening.

However, embodying these three wisdoms by themselves will not enable you to be a centred leader. You need all five points of the star.

We will explore each of the points of the star later in the book, but here's a quick overview of how you can use the star as a guide to becoming a more centred leader.

Inner engagement

Let's start with how you engage internally with yourself.

Emotional agility

Emotional agility means managing your emotions flexibly and healthily. Instead of reacting impulsively, you acknowledge your thoughts and feelings, understand them and choose your response with intention. As a centred leader, you avoid suppressing emotions. You recognise them and decide how to act in alignment with your values.

Emotional agility helps you maintain balance and your composure when the unexpected happens or stress levels escalate. It allows you to make decisions that reflect your principles and the needs of your team. A centred leader uses emotional agility to stay present and make decisions grounded in the current moment rather than getting lost in past mistakes or future worries.

As a centred leader, you respond thoughtfully instead of reacting impulsively. You're a more measured and consistent leader who can develop trusting and respectful relationships. You can also adapt to change, stay aligned with your core values and remain flexible in your approach.

Intellectual flexibility

As a centred leader you use intellectual flexibility to adapt your thinking when faced with confusing, uncertain or unknown situations where new information and different perspectives are emerging or circumstances are changing. This involves questioning assumptions, considering alternative viewpoints and adjusting the approach when needed. However, this flexibility doesn't compromise your values and character strengths. Instead, it ensures that your ideas and resulting actions stay aligned with reality.

Intellectual flexibility allows you to successfully navigate the complexities of leadership with clarity, adaptability and less stress.

A centred leader uses intellectual flexibility to make informed decisions, integrating diverse perspectives and data. You avoid rigid thinking and ground your choices in the current situation. You're open to new ideas, listen without judgment and encourage creativity and innovation.

Flexibly responding with an eye on where the situation is heading and the strategic objective that you're trying to achieve enables you to bounce back when required and stay focused on your long-term goals rather than clinging to outdated methods and what no longer serves you, your team or organisation.

External engagement

The next elements relate to external engagement.

Contextual wisdom

Contextual wisdom means understanding the broader environment in which you operate and applying that understanding to your leadership decisions. It involves recognising that context shapes every decision and action. You continuously scan for emerging trends and shifts, using your intuition and fit-for-purpose tools to interpret the changes and shape the next steps to fit the specific circumstances.

Contextual wisdom allows you to make decisions that are not only informed but also relevant and timely. A leader with contextual wisdom anticipates trends. You see beyond the immediate situation, looking for patterns and trends that might affect your organisation. This foresight allows you to prepare for changes rather than simply reacting to them. You grasp the broader implications of your decisions and consider how they will play out in different contexts, including social, economic or environmental, so that your actions align with your values and longer-term objectives.

As a centred leader you understand that many situations, especially those impacted by people, are more than complicated because they are, in essence, complex. As such, you're always thinking about how your decisions fit into and will be affected by the bigger picture.

Applying your wisdom in context anchors your leadership in the present and enables you to answer the question, 'What's the next right step?'

Inter-relational expertise

Centred leaders use inter-relational expertise to connect with others to foster trust, enable collaboration and make forward progress. Inter-relational expertise involves building strong relationships, resolving conflicts and navigating complex interpersonal dynamics.

As this type of leader, you listen to understand, not just to respond, and you build strong, meaningful relationships across teams, work areas and organisations. This enables open communication and mutual respect even when there are divergent views and competing challenges.

You're able to effectively resolve conflict, adapt to different cultural contexts and inspire others by aligning shared goals with individual contributions. Your interactions are thoughtful and intentional. You know that, while you cannot control all your and other people's experiences, you can actively manage yourself and invite the type of response you desire from others.

This enriches relationships and cultivates empathy and the ability to influence stakeholders positively. A leader with strong inter-relational expertise has a clear tolerance of ambiguity and can create spaces for creativity to flourish. This element of centred leadership is closely connected to emotional agility and demands adaptability, inclusivity and the empowerment of others.

Tactical agility

Tactical agility is closely connected to contextual wisdom as it uses that wisdom to adapt strategies and actions in response to changing circumstances quickly. A centred leader acts insightfully and courageously to navigate uncertainty, making practical, timely decisions that keep the team moving forward. You'll notice when they are getting stuck in inertia and take steps to unlock insight and action. As a centred leader, you understand the need to execute adjustments on the fly, ensuring your leadership remains effective and responsive in dynamic environments.

Following your 5 points

Together, these five points of the Centring Star form your guiding light for centred leadership. They're how you find your way to the eye of the storm so you can get perspective, reconnect with yourself, re-energise and strategise your next step. And in the next chapters we'll dive into how we can really, practically do this.

It's important to remember that nothing is going to stop the storms. The challenges we face are only going to increase. But our goal is to move from the battering winds into the peace that's at the eye of the storm. And we can do that by using our Centring Star to guide ourselves in alignment with our values.

PART 4
INNER
ENGAGEMENT

CHAPTER 5

Centring with Emotional Agility

There was a time when one of my former colleagues thought they were presenting a calm and thoughtful exterior to the people they worked with. In reality, they were holding themselves together so tightly and their emotions were so locked down that their anxious feelings were seeping out all around them.

What they thought was a calm exterior was actually a big flashing warning which told everyone surrounding them to watch out. The people they worked with could see it was only a matter of time before my colleague snapped and started biting people's heads off.

At the time, my colleague didn't understand the inside out nature of leadership. They didn't realise that how you engage with yourself affects how you engage with others.

Centring inside your star

Although each Centring Star is constructed in the same way, it is unique because it reflects the inner world of the leader it is guiding.

Being willing to engage in activities that enable ongoing self-awareness is a prerequisite for staying centred. It's how you stay in touch with your leadership practice and how it affects the people surrounding you and connects to the results you're getting. I like to think of this as staying in touch with your inner star. But how do you actually do this?

Kolb's action-reflection learning model

David Kolb may have developed his action-reflection learning model (also sometimes referred to as a cycle of reflective practice) in the early 1980s[94], but it's stood the test of time. If you don't already have a strategy for maintaining self-awareness as a leader, Kolb's model is a good place to start.

Start with choosing an experience you were directly involved in where you used your leadership skills, then thoughtfully reflect on that experience. You could start with considering:

1. **What specifically happened?** Start by recounting the factual details of the experience without judgement or interpretation to establish a clear baseline of events.

2. **How did you feel during this experience?** Identify and acknowledge the emotions you felt during the event. This will help you understand how these feelings influenced your decisions and actions.

---

94   (19 January 2024). 'Reflective writing: Kolb.' SkillsGuides. University of Hull. https://libguides.hull.ac.uk/reflectivewriting/kolb.

3. **What were the key lessons learned from this experience?** Focus on both the positives and the areas for improvement, reflecting on the underlying lessons.

4. **How do these lessons align with my core values and my strategic objectives?** Evaluate the insights you've gained against your values and strategic objectives.

Once you've finished reflecting, take what you learned from that experience and plan specific actions you could take in future situations. Be specific and thorough.

You may want to set aside time to do this weekly, or if the change you're involved in is highly complex and rapidly evolving, do it daily. You could set the time to do this to align with something you do, like travelling on the train home after work.

Forming a habit of action-reflection learning and continuously applying these insights will enable you to cultivate emotional and cognitive mastery, act authentically and make wiser decisions.

Emotional agility

To stay centred, especially once we venture back out into the storm, we need to be emotionally agile. Our emotions provide valuable data into how we are leading ourselves and others. If you're a leader who, when things get tough, puts a smile on your face and keeps it plastered there no matter what gets thrown at you, this section is a must-read. It's also a must-read if you often think you're doing the right thing by keeping it together in front of your team so find yourself pushing down those feelings into a little compartment inside so you can get through today and onto what's next.

Unfortunately, compartmentalising your feelings won't work in the long term. Those feelings don't go away. It's not in your or anyone else's interest to avoid uncomfortable feelings so that you can keep going. And that's not only because you're missing the important data that those emotions can convey to you.

Emotional agility arises out of psychological flexibility. Clinical psychologists and researchers Todd B. Kashdan and Jonathan Rottenberg define psychological flexibility as:

> 'The measure of how a person:
> 1. *Adapts to fluctuating situational demands;*
> 2. *Reconfigures mental resources;*
> 3. *Shifts perspective; and*
> 4. *Balances competing desires, needs and life domains'.*[95]

In other words, people who are psychologically flexible are able to be fully present in the moment, think about what is happening openly and with curiosity and take steps to advance towards those goals based on that input. These same steps work with our emotions.

Emotions are part of being human. We all have them. It's part of our biology. So, denying our emotions is like denying that we are human. People with controlling tendencies can feel like their emotions are one more thing that needs to be controlled. Instead we need to be able to recognise them in the moment, consider what they are and why they're occurring with curiosity and then take actions based on this information. This is why I find 'emotional agility' is a more useful term than 'emotional regulation' – because we aren't trying to regulate our emotions as much as flexibly respond to them.

---

95   Kashdan, T & Rottenberg, J. (2010). 'Psychological flexibility as a fundamental aspect of health.' *Clinical Psychology Review.* https://doi.org/10.1016/j.cpr.2010.03.0012.

Dr Susan David, a psychologist on the faculty of Harvard Medical School and the co-founder and co-director of the Institute of Coaching at McLean Hospital, has researched and written extensively about emotional agility.

She and her Harvard Business Review co-author Christina Congleton explain that 'we see leaders stumble not because they have undesirable thoughts and feelings—that's inevitable—but because they get hooked by them, like fish caught on a line. This happens in one of two ways. They buy into the thoughts, treating them like facts … and avoid situations that evoke them … Or, usually at the behest of their supporters, they challenge the existence of the thoughts and try to rationalise them away… and perhaps force themselves into similar situations, even when those go against their core values and goals.'[96]

Your emotions are like a weather barometer. They provide you with useful information about how you are experiencing a situation. Knowing your personal triggers enables you to notice when you need to pause and decide on the most effective response. Doing so enhances your ability to thrive through struggle.

Acceptance and commitment therapy

Psychologists Steve Hayes and Kelly Wilson identified that trying to control or avoid painful emotions and thoughts can make them more persistent and distressing.[97] In response, they developed acceptance and commitment therapy, which instead encourages people to accept those painful emotions and thoughts and commit to actions that align with their values.[98]

---

96   David, S & Congleton, C. (November 2013). 'Emotional Agility.' *Harvard Business Review.* https://hbr.org/2013/11/emotional-agility.

97   Hayes, S, Strosahl, K & Wilson, K. (2011). *Acceptance and Commitment Therapy: The Process and Practice of Mindful Change.* Guilford Press.

98   Hayes. Acceptance and Commitment Therapy.

You may be thinking that sounds easier than done. It is like trying to hold a beach ball underwater. It takes constant effort to keep it there. However, eventually the ball pops back up, sometimes unexpectedly and with force. The same thing happens with emotions when you suppress them.

When you accept your feelings with curiosity and kindness, the ball is still there. However, it's now floating on the water's surface, moving with the eddies and currents created by your and other people's actions. When you reduce the tension associated with resisting engaging with your feelings, situations will feel less stressful.

Steve Hayes describes the core aim of ACT as 'contacting the present moment fully as a conscious human being, and, based on what the situation affords, changing or persisting in behaviour in the service of chosen values.'[99]

The core principles of ACT are:

1. **Acceptance**

    Embracing your thoughts and feelings without trying to change them. It's about noticing them and seeing them as data rather than an instruction to behave in a certain way. For example, I notice I am angry instead of aggressively raising my voice. Or I notice and acknowledge that I'm feeling hurt at being ignored rather than withdrawing.

2. **Cognitive Defusion**

    This step is about learning to see your thoughts and feelings as just that – thoughts and feelings. It helps you avoid being captured and dictated to by what you're thinking and feeling and increases your

---

99   Chun-Qing, Z, Leeming, E et al. (11 January 2018). 'Acceptance and Commitment Therapy for Health Behavior Change: A Contextually Driven Approach.' *Frontiers in Psychology.* https://www.ncbi.nlm.nih.gov/pmc/articles/PMC5769281/#:~:text=Psychological%20 flexibility%20is%20described%20as,et%20al.%2C%201996).

capacity to respond to the situation rather than be driven by your own personal chatter.

3. Being Present

When you're present, you fully engage with what's happening right now rather than getting lost in thoughts about the past or worries about the future. It requires tuning into the present moment with all your senses, without judgement or distraction.

4. Self as Context

When you see your 'self as context' you can put yourself at a distance and observe your thoughts and feelings so they don't define you. This enables you to reduce the impact of your experiences and choose how to respond as you see your experiences from a distance.

5. Values

You discover and embrace the things that matter most to you – what you care about deeply and what gives your life meaning.

6. Committed Action

Here you take steps towards living according to your values, even in the face of difficult thoughts and feelings. You don't wait for the perfect moment or for things to feel easy.

So, rather than running away and hiding from or ignoring our feelings, emotional agility requires you to face them, align them with your values and take committed action. And when you do, you're in a position to become a more centred leader.

My former colleague demonstrated this very well when they realised that suppressing their emotions was a mistake. Instead of trying to ignore their feelings, they instead began noting those feelings with curiosity and kindness and then acting on those feelings in alignment with their values.

They also found it helpful to signal to other people that they were dealing with something challenging personally and that it was affecting their mood. They were surprised when expressing their vulnerability prompted a more empathetic and inclusive response from the people who literally used to run the other way when they sensed the vibe my colleague was giving off.

My colleague became a more centred leader by using emotional agility to stay present and make decisions grounded in the current moment rather than getting lost in past mistakes or future worries.

Getting the balance right

In the last few years of my executive career people kept saying things that made it feel like I would let everyone let down if I stopped long enough to give my repressed emotions any air. The problem was that each time I pushed the many negative emotions down, and plastered a smile on my face, I was unknowingly tending to a fire-filled pit of lava deep inside.

During the two years I tried to keep those feelings locked down, the internal pressures built up and built up until, eventually, the pressure had to find a way out, just like lava overflowing from a volcano.

In my case (and in many cases), the internal pressure pushed those feelings out in a physical way. Remember the tears inexplicably rolling down my face? This was a classic case of reaping the rewards of emotional avoidance.

Ignoring negative emotions is like an ostrich burying its head in the sand to avoid danger. While the ostrich might feel safer, it's not fooling the lion creeping up behind. Ignoring the lion doesn't make them disappear, and ignoring the negative emotions won't make them disappear either. It just blinds us to the reality that we're about to be eaten.

Instead of automatically plastering a smile on your face, I encourage you to go deeper and look for the positive emotional attractors (PEAs).[100] The PEAS are the positive feelings and visions that can inspire and motivate you to move towards your aspirations.[101] When you tap into those PEAs, you are more likely to be pulled towards what you want to achieve without having to push so hard. This doesn't mean ignoring the negative emotions. In fact, effective leadership requires finding a balance between positive and negative emotional attractors (NEAs), but it's not a straight one-to-one ratio.

The positivity ratio

University of North Carolina, Chapel Hill Professor Barbara Fredrickson developed the 'positivity ratio.'[102] She suggested experiencing positive emotions in a three-to-one ratio with negative emotions leads to a tipping point beyond which we naturally become more resilient to adversity and better able to achieve our potential.[103]

She says that 'when we inject people with positivity, their outlook expands. They see the big picture. When we inject them with neutrality or negativity, their peripheral vision shrinks. There is no big picture, no dots to connect.'[104]

---

100 Fredrickson, B. (2001). 'The role of positive emotions in positive psychology: The broaden-and-build theory of positive emotions.' *American Psychologist.* https://doi. org/10.1037/0003-066X.56.3.218.

101 Fredrickson. The role of positive emotions in positive psychology.

102 Fredrickson, B. (2013). 'Updated thinking on positivity ratios.' *American Psychologist.* https://doi.org/10.1037/a0033584.

103 Fredrickson. Updated thinking on positivity ratios.

104 Fredrickson. Updated thinking on positivity ratios.

Although the exact ratio has been criticised, the rule of thumb, backed by sound evidence, is that a greater positivity ratio leads to better health, thinking and social experience.[105]

Professor Richard Boyatzis from Case Western Reserve University has undertaken extensive research with leaders about PEAs, NEAs, chronic stress and what enables our renewal. In other words, things that bring us back towards positive emotions or PEAs. In the book, *Helping People Change*, Boyatzis and his co-authors explain that when stress and NEAs are unavoidable, we can turn to activities that 'renew us' to pull back towards PEAs.[106] However, both the variety and dosage of renewal activities are important.

Their research recognised the importance of exercise but also highlighted that you need more than exercise to experience renewal. Renewal activities need to be frequent, not lengthy, and a greater variety of activities is better[107].

The next time you think of spending even more time at the gym or extending your morning walk to manage your stress, consider that Boyatzis' research found that you would be better off breaking a one-hour renewal activity into four separate, 15-minute activities throughout the day.[108] So, instead of extending the time spent pounding the treadmill or pavement, you could choose to spend 15 minutes talking to upbeat friends, 15 minutes doing yoga or meditation, 15 minutes playing with your kids or pets, 15 minutes laughing with other people or any combination of activities that help refill your cup.

---

105 Diehl, M et al. (23 May 2011). 'The Ratio between Positive and Negative Affect and Flourishing Mental Health across Adulthood.' *Aging Mental Health*. https://www.ncbi.nlm. nih.gov/pmc/articles/PMC3158962/.

106 Boyatzis, R, Smith, M & Van Oosten, E. (2019). *Helping People Change: Coaching with Compassion for Lifelong Learning and Growth*. Harvard Business Press.

107 Boyatzis. Helping People Change.

108 Boyatzis. Helping People Change.

Remember, it's not about eliminating negative emotions but learning to manage them in a more agile way while focusing on the positive.

Practising mindful acceptance

Russ Harris, an Australian physician and author, has also written extensively on ACT. He recommends practising 'mindful acceptance.'[109]

Mindful acceptance means acknowledging and accepting emotions rather than trying to avoid or suppress them. It also recognises that emotions are not necessarily 'true' or indicative of reality. Instead of trying to change or eliminate them, you observe them with curiosity and openness, without judgement or criticism.[110]

Russ Harris compares our unwanted thoughts to heavy iron chains, which weigh us down and make it difficult to move forward with ease. When we unconsciously respond to our thoughts they can be like physical restraints, holding us back. However, when we treat thoughts as only words linked together, they lose their power.[111]

Take a leaf out of my former colleague's book and remember that ignoring your feelings won't make them go away. They'll find a way to come out eventually. Often when they're least welcome, just like that lava in a volcano. Instead of beating yourself up when you have negative feelings, or smashing them down, take the advice of Kristin Neff, a world-leading researcher on compassion and founder of the Mindful Self-Compassion program, and 'treat yourself with the same kindness you would treat a friend.'[112]

---

109 Harris, R. (2022). *The Happiness Trap: How to Stop Struggling and Start Living.* Shambhala.
110 Harris. The Happiness Trap.
111 Harris. The Happiness Trap.
112 Neff, K. (2011). *Self-Compassion: The Proven Power of Being Kind to Yourself.* William Morrow.

Mindfulness and emotional agility

'The greatest weapon against stress is our ability to choose one thought over another'.

This quote is attributed to William James, often referred to as the father of American psychology. Although it's not actually a direct quote but a common paraphrase of ideas from his body of work, it reminds us to approach our leadership mindfully rather than mindlessly.

If you haven't realised it yet, mindfulness is an essential tool for developing emotional agility.

Mindfulness can be achieved without having to start a daily meditation practice. Dr Ellen Langer, a Professor of Psychology at Harvard University who has been referred to as the mother of mindfulness, defines mindfulness as 'the simple act of actively noticing things'.[113]

Are you starting to get a sense of how important it is to manage our thoughts?

Langer's approach is very down to earth and definitely not 'woo woo'. Her research on the benefits of mindfulness has been developed using Western science and social psychological perspectives.[114] According to Langer, mindfulness involves being fully aware and present without judgment. It isn't about ignoring negative thoughts or replacing them with positive ones. Instead, mindfulness helps you observe your thoughts and emotions with

---

113 Tippett, K. (Host). Langer, E. (29 May 2014). Science of Mindlessness and Mindfulness. (No. 552) [Audio podcast episode]. In On Being. On Being Studios. https://podcasts. apple.com/us/podcast/ellen-langer-science-of-mindlessness-and-mindfulness/ id150892556?i=1000394341878.

114 Langer, E & Ngnoumen, C. (2017). 'Mindfulness.' In D Dunn (Ed.), *Positive Psychology*. Routledge.

kindness, and without deciding whether they are good or bad – just allowing that they exist.[115]

Her research found that mindfulness offers many benefits, such as better health, increased awareness of different perspectives and enhanced problem-solving skills. It also helps people gain greater control over their thoughts in both their personal and professional lives.[116]

Langer's research shows that being mindful rather than mindless makes leaders more adaptable, flexible and open to new information, which can result in more effective and innovative leadership.[117] Put simply, mindfulness is like driving a car. Your mind is the driver, and your body is the car. To drive well, you need to pay attention to the car's condition, like fuel levels and warning lights. In the same way, mindfulness helps you stay aware of your body and emotions, allowing you to perform at your best.

When you practise mindfulness you'll find it easier to centre yourself in the eye of the storm. As a leader it will improve your ability to interact with others, maintain a balanced perspective and notice the emotions of your team members. Mindful leaders also tend to be more self-aware and take better care of themselves, which will boost your resilience and capacity to handle challenges.[118]

This is something that Google realised a long time ago. In 2007, Chade-Meng Tan, one of Google's first engineers, noticed something important. His coworkers were smart and successful, but they were also stressed. Meng knew there was a way to help, and this idea led to the creation of the Search

---

115 Langer, E. (2015). *Mindfulness: 25th Anniversary Edition*. De Capo Lifelong Books.

116 Langer. *Mindfulness*.

117 Langer. *Mindfulness*.

118 Chesley, J & Wylson, A. (2016). 'Ambiguity: the emerging impact of mindfulness for change leaders.' *Journal of Change Management*. https://www.researchgate.net/publication/309147830_Ambiguity_the_emerging_impact_of_mindfulness_for_change_leaders.

Inside Yourself (SIY) program.[119] Designed within Google, SIY used simple practices from mindfulness and emotional intelligence to help employees handle stress and improve their focus.

SIY quickly became popular at Google. Employees who went through the program reported being better at handling daily challenges and feeling more engaged at work. They learned to manage their reactions and understand others' emotions, which made teamwork smoother. Seeing the success, Meng and experts Philippe Goldin and Marc Lesser decided to offer SIY to more people. In 2012, they set up the Search Inside Yourself Leadership Institute, or SIYLI, to reach beyond Google.[120]

SIY at Google shows us that there is value in slowing down and paying attention. There's no quick fix and taking a tokenistic approach to mindfulness isn't the answer. For anyone interested in understanding this approach better, the Search Inside Yourself Leadership Institute offers plenty of resources and detailed descriptions of its methods and results.

Mindfulness or meditation?

Mindfulness techniques are valuable tools. However, some studies suggest that workplace well-being programs that focus on mindfulness meditation have varied impacts depending on the type of meditation practised.[121] Those studies explored two key types of meditation:

1. **Breath-based mediation.** Breath-based meditation boosted cognitive empathy but might lower feelings of guilt, potentially affecting people's level of personal accountability.

---

119 'Origins.' Search Inside Yourself. https://siyli.org/.
120 https://siyli.org/
121 Cameron, L & Hafenbrack, A. (12 December 2022). 'Research: When Mindfulness Does – and Doesn't – Help at Work.' *Harvard Business Review.* https://hbr.org/2022/12/research-when-mindfulness-does-and-doesnt-help-at-work.

2. **Loving-kindness mediation.** Loving-kindness meditation enhanced emotional empathy, making it ideal for roles that require high social interaction and genuine emotional connection.[122]

Their findings suggest that jobs involving lots of interpersonal interaction would likely benefit from both meditation types, rather than just focusing on breath work. Of course, if we go back to Dr Ellen Langer's definition of mindfulness, we're reminded that being mindful doesn't have to include meditation. It's just one tool that can help us to actively notice things like our own emotions.[123] And it can bring certain additional benefits depending on the situation in which we find ourselves leading.

Mindfulness is particularly useful during high-stress moments or when deep focus and empathy are needed. It prepares you for challenging meetings, managing emotional conversations and sparking innovation under pressure. Research also confirms that mindfulness can be protective, helping leaders to sustain attention and manage stress in high-pressure environments like the military.[124]

If you have to deal with situations that are confusing, uncertain or unknown – and we know that you will in today's VUCA world – mindfulness has been consistently proven to have the highest, positive correlation with tolerating sitting in the discomfort created by ambiguity. It helps you to build comfort with ambiguity, develop a desire for challenging work and

---

122 Cameron. Research: When Mindfulness Does – and Doesn't – Help at Work.

123 Langer. Science of Mindlessness and Mindfulness.

124 Jha, A, et al. (21 January 2016). 'Practice is protective: Mindfulness training promotes cognitive resilience in high-stress cohorts.' Mindfulness. https://link.springer.com/article/10.1007/s12671-015-0465-9; Jha, A et al. (4 April 2019). 'Deploying Mindfulness to Gain Cognitive Advantage: Considerations for Military Effectiveness and Well-being.' NATO Science and Technology Conference Proceedings. https://repository.law.miami.edu/fac_articles/1091/; Myers, M. (1 June 2015). 'Improving Military Resilience through Mindfulness Training. U.S. Army. https://www.army.mil/article/149615/improving_military_resilience_through_mindfulness_training.

manage uncertainty for yourself and those around you.[125] If you had to choose between the eight skills the evidence tells us will enable you to build a tolerance of ambiguity (more on that later!), mindfulness would come out as the skill with the greatest likelihood of delivering a positive impact.[126]

Emotional agility is just the beginning

Exploring your emotional agility is about being willing to engage internally and respond to your emotions with curiosity, kindness and a commitment to your own values. By building your emotional agility, you're laying the foundation for leading with authenticity and awareness. However, to navigate our complex world, and lead through the challenges this presents, emotional agility needs to be supported by intellectual flexibility as well.

125 [Citation TBD]

126 O'Connor, P et al. (8 November 2021). 'Leader Tolerance of Ambiguity: Implications for Follower Performance Outcomes in High and Low Ambiguous Work Situations.' *The Journal of Applied Behavioral Science.* https://journals.sagepub.com/doi/abs/10.1177/00218863211053676; O'Connor, P, Becker, K & Fewster, K. (10 August 2018). 'Tolerance of ambiguity at work predicts leadership, job performance, and creativity.' *Creating Uncertainty Conference.* https://eprints.qut.edu.au/120614/.

CHAPTER 6

Centring with Intellectual Flexibility

In 2010, the San José copper mine in Chile collapsed, trapping 33 miners deep underground, with half a million tons of rock blocking the mine's entrance.[127] Initially, the miners' rescue was not even thought possible. They were in a perilous situation with scarce food and unstable conditions, but they held on for 69 days. It was an incredible story of ingenuity and teamwork as experts came together from across the world to save them.

Rescue teams had to think on their feet, constantly adapting their strategies as new information came in. They tried different methods, learning from each failure and improving their plans. How they approached these challenges required flexible thinking, enabling them to turn what seemed like an impossible mission into a remarkable rescue.

---

127 Corrigan. M. (29 October 2014). 'The Incredible Story Of Chilean Miners Rescued From The 'Deep Down Dark'.' [Audio]. NPR.org. https://www.npr.org/2014/10/29/359839104/the-incredible-story-of-chilean-miners-rescued-from-the-deep-down-dark#:~:text=On%20Oct.,raised%20by%20a%20giant%20crane.

The story of the miners' rescue shows how adaptable thinking and teamwork can overcome even the toughest challenges. It also provided leadership lessons that can be applied to problem-solving in any field. Amy Edmondson, the Novartis Professor of Leadership and Management at Harvard Business School, has written about how the rescue was only possible because a group of people with a diverse range of perspectives came together to produce innovation, and the leaders who enabled it.[128]

The value of tapping into diverse, multiple perspectives when dealing with complexity is well documented.[129] However, before that can happen, a leader needs to first tap into their own intellectual flexibility and create the conditions to unleash new possibilities, innovations or solutions to highly-complex problems.

You may not be faced with a Chilean mine disaster, but when leading during times of complex change, you will continually face your own versions of challenges that may seem insurmountable. At those times, engaging in more flexible thinking will enable you to be a more centred leader who can decide on the next right thing to do.

---

128 Rashid, F, Edmondson, A & Leonard, H. (2013). 'Leadership Lessons from the Chilean Mine Rescue.' *Harvard Business Review.* https://hbr.org/2013/07/leadership-lessons-from-the-chilean-mine-rescue.

129 Berger, J & Johnston, K. (2015). *Simple habits for complex times: Powerful practices for leaders.* Stanford University Press.

Intellectual flexibility

We've already covered the importance of accepting and managing how you feel – the point of the star focused on your inner emotional world. Now, we're going to move to how you think – not your team, but you. Because when you're leading through complex change, everything you do, including everything you think, creates ripples. These ripples can enable and create new possibilities, or they can build in momentum to become waves that overwhelm and swamp your people and opportunities.

Just like noticing your emotions can open up new possibilities and reduce stress, so can noticing how you think and respond to situations. And this can help you focus on creating ripples of positive change.

Being intellectually flexible means changing your thinking and adapting quickly to new situations, challenges or information. It means being open to new ideas, methods and strategies when needed to achieve the best results. So the question then becomes, how to become more intellectually flexible?

How you choose to show up matters

I once attended an interstate conference believing I was completely organised. My travel and accommodation were booked, and I knew what sessions I would attend. I was confident everything was in hand... until it wasn't.

I tried to check in to the accommodation I had paid for through the professional conference organiser. Unfortunately, I discovered that the hotel had no idea who I was and that it was full.

Luckily, I had the conference organiser's mobile number, but that's when the real frustration began. They started by apologising that they had missed my booking and for failing to respond to the two emails I sent them before I arrived.

However, they seemed to ignore that I was standing at reception, needing three nights' accommodation I'd already paid for. They then proceeded to tell me I could pay for higher-priced accommodation elsewhere and that they would refund me the difference between what I had already paid after the conference.

As you can imagine, I wasn't too keen on just hoping the conference organiser refunded me the difference in accommodation costs based on a phone call. Especially since he hadn't met his obligations already.

Unfortunately for the conference organiser, I was not prepared to make his life as easy as possible, which he clearly expected. His response made it clear he thought I was being unreasonable.

After more than an hour and many phone calls with the conference organiser, I received help from another person from the professional association convening the conference. I finally had a room in the original hotel despite his lack of efforts. It was a good example of how not to treat a customer.

So, where did the conference organiser go wrong?

He assumed his way was the only way and failed to explore the issue from anyone else's perspective. Apart from being appalling customer service, it was like he was driving with blinders on, only able to see his perspective and ignoring all the other opportunities to resolve the problem.

Thankfully, someone else asked the hotel curious questions and discovered that a room could be made available. The person from the professional association persisted in the face of obstacles, used his curiosity to learn how the challenge could be overcome and discovered a useful insight about hotel bookings he could use when he was the conference convenor the following year. He had what Carol Dweck would call a growth mindset.[130]

The original conference organiser likely never heard what the Dalai Lama is widely reported to have said, namely, 'When you talk, you are only repeating what you already know. But if you listen, you may learn something new.'

Adopt a beginner's mind

Another way we can develop some intellectual flexibility is by adopting a beginner's mind. But what does this mean? We can explain it by returning to the sea. Imagine you're a seasoned captain navigating a familiar route. You've sailed this path many times successfully. Confidently, you steer your ship through waters that feel like home. But one day, the currents change unexpectedly, and the maps you've always trusted no longer guide you. Struggling against the new tide, you try to get back on course using your old strategies. Unfortunately, clinging to what used to work stops you from moving forward, and you miss reaching port by the required time.

If only you had adopted a beginner's mind!

In Zen Buddhism, the concept of a 'beginner's mind,' or 'shoshin,' encourages approaching situations with openness, eagerness and a lack of preconceptions – much like a novice encountering something for the first time.[131] It requires us to stay open to new experiences and insights and set aside the rigidity of past knowledge.[132]

---

130 Dweck. What Having a "Growth Mindset" Actually Means.

131 Suzuki, S. (1970). *Zen Mind, Beginner's Mind: Informal Talks on Zen Meditation and Practice.* Weatherhill.

132 Suzuki. Zen Mind, Beginner's Mind.

As the Zen monk Shunryu Suzuki eloquently puts it, 'In the beginner's mind there are many possibilities, but in the expert's mind there are few.'[133]

During crises, whether financial or reputational, or natural disasters, leaders must have a beginner's mind. When you do, it will help you avoid relying on potentially outdated crisis management plans and instead assess the situation with fresh eyes. This enables you to develop solutions specifically tailored to the immediate circumstances.

There are many other complex changes where a beginner's mind is valuable. You may be considering entering a new market, developing a new product or service, implementing a new technology or undergoing a merger and acquisition. Each of these can benefit from taking a fresh look at how to approach these opportunities.

In particular, mergers and acquisitions often fail due to a lack of sensitivity to the merging cultures and systems. Leaders who adopt a beginner's mind can more objectively assess the strengths and weaknesses of both entities to integrate the best practices from each.

It can be useful to approach how we think about complex change, as a sculptor would approach an uncarved wood block. They might know what they want to create, but they must also adapt as they work, responding to the wood as it takes shape. Similarly, a leader with a beginner's mind sees opportunities where others see obstacles, without being held back by what they think they already know.

---

133 Suzuki. Zen Mind, Beginner's Mind.

Avoid assuming people who disagree with you are wrong

'It isn't what happens to you, but how you react that matters'.
– Epictetus, Greek Stoic philosopher[134]

Years ago, a boss decided to give me some very direct feedback at the end of a weekly catch-up meeting. No one likes hearing they're not meeting their boss's expectations, and I certainly didn't. My first response was that the criticism was unfair – all the work they said they were concerned about was on track and, when they stated that I was too often late to meetings, I felt wronged and misunderstood.

However, I then took a breath and chose to look at it from her perspective. I got curious about where she was coming from and why it was reasonable for her to feel the way she did. It suddenly started to make more sense. I had fallen into the trap of not adjusting how I managed upwards when my former boss moved on.

The work was on track, but the new boss wanted more frequent updates. There was also some truth to being late to meetings. I wasn't late to all my meetings, but I had been late to a few she attended.

When I could think about my boss's concerns more flexibly and not give in to those immediate fight, flight or freeze emotions, how to improve the situation became clearer. It was a relief when she was happy that her concerns were listened to, and she could see positive change. Digging into those feelings and getting uncomfortable had been worth it.

---

134 Epictetus. (2008). *The Enchiridion.* (E. Carter & T. W. Higginson, Trans.). Dover Publications.

Now imagine that situation on a broader scale. Customers or the public believe something is a problem. However, you feel their perception is unfair, or worse still, you write their opinion off as ill-informed.

Nothing is done, and the situation gets worse. It becomes a stand-off where both sides feel they're right, and the others are wrong. It blows up and becomes an even bigger problem with stakeholders who are fired up and ready to fight. This is not a winning situation for anyone.

On the other hand, when we're more agile in our thinking and seek data from diverse sources, it allows us and others to 'stand back to see the bigger picture' before stepping towards the detail and the solution. Flexible thinking allows us to respond to emerging issues earlier and then helps us to keep adapting until we can find a way through change, uncertainty or ambiguity.

It's like you're a human GPS recalculating new routes every time there's a roadblock. You don't just see one path; you see all the hidden shortcuts, back alleys and scenic routes. And when you have more data you can make the adjustments you need in the moment to keep you on the best path to your destination. However, it's important not to refer to *all* data. If you wait to understand everything and gather everything you'll never have enough. And that will just see you stuck in analysis paralysis.

If you have perfectionist tendencies, flexible thinking is about synthesising data and information to the point where you can realistically expect success. You don't want to keep bouncing around until you find the perfect path. It's better to get on a path and work out how to make early sense of whether it's heading in the right direction, so you have time to adapt.

Flexibility for influence

Flexible thinking also opens possibilities when you lack control.

Jennifer Riel, who teaches at the Rotman School of Management in Toronto, shared the example of LEGO wanting to be involved in making an awesome movie that was also really good for LEGO as a brand.[135]

The CEO realised he couldn't control the creatives but could influence what happened before work started on the movie. So he got the movie makers to spend time with LEGO's most committed, fanatical customers. He hoped that by getting the moviemakers to understand what LEGO meant to these customers, they too would fall in love with LEGO and, therefore, protect the brand. As a result, the movie makers discovered things like how evil it is to use glue in the LEGO community. They were then able to build these elements into the plotline to create a better, more engaging movie that also protected the brand.[136]

Reframing problems

Intellectual flexibility also helps you to reframe problems which can open up new possibilities in terms of solutions and outcomes. In the mid-2000s, I worked on the 'Alert Doctors' project with doctors who believed they needed less sleep than the average person. We engaged a university, involved the doctors in action-based research and tracked their sleep patterns. The study proved they were not physiologically different from the rest of the community.

---

135 Bates, H. (Host). Riel, J. (28 June 2023). Solving Problems with Integrative Thinking. (No. 12) [Audio podcast episode]. In HBR on Strategy. Harvard Business Review. https://hbr. org/podcast/2023/06/solving-problems-with-integrative-thinking.
136 Bates. Solving Problems with Integrative Thinking.

That was the easy part. The hard part was changing work practices and expectations about how doctors work and take breaks to keep patients safe. We had to continually zig and zag as new challenges and barriers confronted us. Eventually, we could see a positive shift compared to the previous twelve months. We learned the importance of stepping off the path you're on and shifting how you look at problems.

Instead of focusing on solutions underpinned by assumptions about what the problem is, we should experiment with reframing the problem. Downtown Dog Rescue in Los Angeles reframed how they looked at the lack of people adopting the dogs in their shelter. Instead of seeking to have more pets adopted, they focused on why dogs were entering shelters in the first place.[137]

When the problem was reframed from 'people give up their dogs because they are heartless' to 'people give up their dogs because of poverty' the shelter discovered 75% of people experiencing poverty-related barriers wanted to keep their pets and chose to do so when offered help. Reframing gave them an opportunity to solve the problem from a new and more successful angle.

When I look back at the Alert Doctors project, I realise we implemented several reframing practices as well. We involved well-known and respected doctors in action research. We created legitimacy by strapping monitors to the wrists of doctors that other doctors trusted. We permitted those doctors to be curious and invite other people to share their experiences.

The research was facilitated by world-renowned sleep experts who could expand the project boundaries into a high-pressure health context because of their previous experience with the military. Medical administrators could speak freely because their jobs were not at risk. However, the external experts stopped them from getting stuck in old ways by stimulating them to think

---

137 Wedell-Wedellsborg, T. (2017). 'Are You Solving the Right Problem?' *Harvard Business Review.* https://hbr.org/2017/01/are-you-solving-the-right-problems.

differently. We also stayed curious about what would motivate doctors to feel they could take a break from work.

A big breakthrough came when we realised the problem was not about sleep. It was about how the doctors' commitment to their patients often overrode their other needs and desires, like spending time with their family and friends. Reframing the problem made doctors feel less like they were the problem and allowed everyone to focus on removing barriers that prevented them from living a more well-rounded life.

Thomas Wedell-Wedellsborg who wrote about Downtown Dog Rescue says, 'You won't know which problems can benefit from being reframed until you try'.[138] Reframing problems is like looking at a Rubik's Cube from a different angle. It is still the same cube, but that new perspective might just be what you need to come up with different solutions. And this comes down to embracing intellectual flexibility.

Time and space matter

Imagine driving to meet a client. You've visited their office multiple times, but today you arrive at the old location only to remember that they recently moved premises. Your mind was on other things, so you easily slipped into autopilot, relying on old thinking patterns and reacting without being fully aware.

Thinking slow, or deliberate thinking, stops you from getting stuck in established patterns that can send you off course. It allows for a mindful approach to decision-making, giving you room to observe, analyse and respond thoughtfully rather than reacting impulsively.

---

138 Wedell-Wedellsborg. Are You Solving the Right Problem?

In his book *Thinking, Fast and Slow*, Nobel prize winning psychologist Daniel Kahneman describes a general 'law of least effort' that applies to both thinking and physical activities.[139] This law suggests that when there are multiple ways to achieve the same result, people will naturally choose the path that requires the least effort.[140] Essentially, our inclination towards laziness is deeply ingrained in us, but the practice of slow thinking aims to challenge this natural tendency.

Reacting based on established patterns is like running through a maze as quick as you can without thinking. You might get out quickly by chance, but you'll probably hit many walls and dead ends. However, if you slow down, look at your surroundings, and think about your choices, you'll have a better chance of finding the true path without getting lost.

Fast and slow thinking is the same. When you rush through a complex problem or situation without taking the time to ruminate, you might make a lucky guess and solve it, but you'll often make mistakes and get stuck. This is because, as Kahneman says, 'We can be blind to the obvious, and we are also blind to our blindness'.[141]

In essence, slow thinking means taking deliberate, thoughtful steps rather than rushing and relying on habits or instincts. From a practical standpoint, to do this you must first decide on the importance of what you're looking at to assess the significance of the issue at hand. Is it a minor inconvenience or a critical challenge? Will it impact the organisation, or just a single team?

Once you've understood this point, it's time to slow it down to suit the context and importance. Not all decisions require the same level of deliberation.

---

139 Kahneman, D. (2011). *Thinking, Fast and Slow*. Farrar, Straus and Giroux.
140 Kahneman. Thinking, Fast and Slow.
141 Kahneman. Thinking, Fast and Slow.

Adjust your thinking speed according to the situation's complexity and importance.

Breaking free from automatic reactions allows you to assess situations more accurately, and make well-informed decisions. And these are the hallmarks of a centred leader.

Trusting your gut

Intellectual flexibility opens us up to different viewpoints and helps us to have better intuition as a leader. On the other hand, when we shut out differing viewpoints, we're setting up our intuitive gut to be faulty.

Isolating ourselves from new ideas or challenging perspectives creates an echo chamber. Because we're only having our own thinking echoed back to us, it skews our insights, and this then constrains our ability to make informed decisions and respond effectively.

Michael Shermer, founder of The Skeptics Society, is reported to have said, 'Being deeply knowledgeable on one subject narrows one's focus and increases confidence, but it also blurs dissenting views until they are no longer visible, thereby transforming data collection into bias confirmation and morphing self-deception into self-assurance.'

Feeding our 'gut feelings' a diversity of experiences and perspectives leads to more accurate insights and decisions because we are more likely to notice and then question the pieces that don't fit our beliefs. It's no different to how our physical gut thrives on probiotics. Being open to a wide range of opinions ultimately fine-tunes our intuitive capabilities.

And we know it works. Steve Jobs was famous for following his gut. Those gut calls contributed to many Apple success stories. But when he was diagnosed with a rare neuroendocrine tumour cancer, Jobs' trust in his intuition led him down a risky path because he chose to prioritise options other than surgery.[142] That decision initially excluded specialist medical care that could have been integrated with the alternative treatments he chose to follow. Because he didn't listen to the wide range of advice available, he was perhaps not able to really trust his gut – which simply didn't have all the information. Unfortunately, this may have contributed to what some doctors described as an unnecessarily early death.

Tapping into intuition has led to business success and even saved lives. However, Job's story shows that previous intuitive success doesn't mean your intuition will always be right.

Intuition versus instinct

Intuition and instincts are often confused, but they are not the same. Instincts are innate, automatic responses like fighting, fleeing or freezing when faced with a threat. These responses are hardwired into our biology and don't require conscious thought. If you're like me, your instincts are why you unconsciously react when you see a request to ID a snake on your local Facebook community page.

On the other hand, intuition can feel like a 'gut feeling' or hunch that guides our decisions. It arises without the need for conscious reasoning, but it steers us towards future opportunities, and can unconsciously protect us from current threats.

---

142 (21 October 2011). 'Steve Jobs Regretted Delaying Cancer Surgery 9 Months, Biographer Says.' *ABC News.* https://abcnews.go.com/Technology/steve-jobs-treatment-biographer-jobs-delayed-surgery-pancreatic/story?id=14781250.

In his book *The Intuition Toolkit: The New Science of Knowing What without Knowing Why*, cognitive neuroscientist Joel Pearson explores the boundaries of intuition and when it might lead us down a wrong or valuable path.[143] According to Pearson, intuition draws on our accumulated knowledge and experiences, often operating below our conscious awareness and subtly influencing our decisions. And he argues that intuition can guide us in situations we know well.[144]

However, our intuition and instincts might not be enough in new or high-stakes situations – like making personal health decisions. We might rely on patterns that don't apply, leading to decisions that feel right but are wrong in the end – much like Jobs.

Warren Buffett once said, 'It's better to be approximately right than precisely wrong.'[145] The key is to know when our intuition is approximately right and when it's leading us astray.[146]

So, how do we know when to trust our gut and how to build better intuition?

143 Pearson, J. (2024). *The Intuition Toolkit: The New Science of Knowing What without Knowing Why*. Simon & Schuster Australia.

144 Pearson. *The Intuition Toolkit*.

145 Buffett, W & Cunningham, L. (Ed.). (2021). *The essays of Warren Buffett: Lessons for corporate America*. Carolina Academic Press.

146 Buffett. *The essays of Warren Buffett*.

The SMILE model developed by Joel Pearson is a guide to understanding whether it's safe to practice intuition in your specific context:

SMILE Model[147]

- **Self-awareness:** Be aware of your emotions. Some positive emotions are okay but avoid using your intuition if your emotions are too high.

- **Mastery:** If you're still learning, avoid using your intuition and be aware mastery is influenced by the process through which you learn rather than how many hours you spend learning. For example, you may only need to experience something negative once rather than spend 10,000 hours learning why it's negative.

- **Impulses and addiction:** If what you're experiencing is an impulse or craving – avoid using your intuition. People living with addiction should always avoid trusting their intuition.

- **Low probability:** Avoid using intuition if probabilistic thinking is required. If you 'know' this is your week to win Powerball the odds are the price of the Lotto ticket would be better spent paying a bill.

- **Environment:** Avoid using your intuition if the situation is unfamiliar, unpredictable, or producing random patterns.

By following Pearson's simple model, you can build your intuitive muscle and make smarter decisions as you navigate between your storms – even when they're converging.

---

147 Pearson, J. (2024). *The Intuition Toolkit: The New Science of Knowing What without Knowing Why.* Simon & Schuster Australia.

Curiosity and intellectual flexibility

'Growth and comfort do not coexist.'
Ginny Rometty, former CEO of IBM[148]

A few years ago, I remember asking my partner why he didn't 'Google it' before deciding to rip out the wall of our internal stairwell, douse it in insect spray and wrap what remained in cling wrap.

Why had he done that? He had discovered termite damage.

But it was only when he did ask Google that he discovered he should have left it alone and called in the experts. This lack of curiosity had consequences, but why it happened is entirely understandable.

In the book *I, Human: AI, Automation and the Quest to Reclaim What Makes Us Unique*, psychologist Tomas Chamorro-Premuzic explains our evolutionary history and provides little incentive for us to develop our curiosity. [149] In our early evolution, curious hunter-gatherers had an increased risk of getting lost, being left behind by the tribe or bringing back less-than-welcome diseases and parasites the tribe's immune systems were unprepared to cope with. They simply couldn't afford to explore new places.

Today we may still want to avoid novel viruses, but the world we live in is extremely different. And today, we don't have the same issues when it comes to being curious. In an interview, futurist Martin Ford shared how, as AI replaces jobs, new jobs will be created that require new skills. This will demand curiosity or what has also been described as learnability.[150]

148 Nusca, A. (8 October 2014). 'IBM's Rometty: 'Growth and comfort don't coexist'.' *Fortune.* https://fortune.com/2014/10/07/ibms-rometty-growth-and-comfort-dont-coexist/.

149 Chamorro-Premuzic, T. (2023). *I, Human: AI, Automation, and the Quest to Reclaim What Makes Us Unique.* Harvard Business Review Press.

150 Mills, A. (26 September 2017). 'Rise of the Robots: Interview with Martin Ford.' Michigan Tech. https://www.mtu.edu/unscripted/2017/09/rise-robots-interview-martin-ford.html.

When we are truly open to learning, we turn off our autopilot and intentionally slow down our thinking to be more curious about our actions, biases, assumptions, motivations or how and why we and others naturally make sense of things.

As Marie Curie said, 'Nothing in life is to be feared, it is only to be understood. Now is the time to understand more, so that we may fear less.'[151] But when we use the same routine questions, we understand less (and so we fear more). It's like reading the same book repeatedly – you know the story well, but there are no new chapters to discover.

Avoiding looking like an ass

Most people have heard the phrase 'when you assume, you make an ass out of "you" and "me"'. This was certainly the case in 2010 when 1,167 retired military officers wrote an open letter to President Barack Obama, who was considering repealing the law that banned gays and lesbians from serving openly in the military.[152]

Those retired officers used their perspective-taking ability to imagine the consequences for current soldiers if the law was repealed. They expressed their strong opposition because their imagining led them to predict that changing the law would 'eventually break the all-volunteer defence force'.[153]

The then-president of the Center for Military Readiness backed them and said, 'They have a lot of military experience, and they know what they're talking about.' In other words, they are the experts, and they know best.

---

151 Benarde, M. (1973). *Our Precarious Habitat*. Norton.

152 Belkin, A. (20 September 2012). 'One Year Out: An Assessment of DADT Repeal's Impact on Military Readiness.' [Report]. Palm Center. https://www.palmcenter.org/wp-content/uploads/2017/12/One-Year-Out_0.pdf.

153 Belkin. One Year Out: An Assessment of DADT Repeal's Impact on Military Readiness.

However, the Pentagon decided to find out for themselves and subsequently undertook one of the largest studies in military history.[154] They directly asked serving soldiers and their spouses what they thought about the 'don't ask, don't tell' policy, and what might happen if it was repealed. They got a very different answer.

The survey of 115,052 soldiers and 44,266 spouses expressed few concerns, with 70% indicating they believed that repealing the policy would have no impact. Of the 69% who indicated they had already worked with a gay service member, 92% said it had no effect or a positive impact on team cohesion.[155]

Unsurprisingly, the law was repealed, and a later study found that one year after its commencement, the law change was a non-event. What would have happened if they'd just relied on what they 'assumed' to be the truth?

Nick Epley, a University of Chicago professor who has devoted most of his career to social cognition, or how people make inferences about other people's thoughts and intentions, says, 'If your belief about the other side's perspective is mistaken, then carefully considering that person's perspective will only magnify the mistake's consequences.'[156]

His research has confirmed there's more value in perspective-*getting* than perspective-taking. The difference between perspective-getting and perspective-taking is that perspective-getting involves getting another person's perspective directly and understanding the mind of the person

---

154 Democratic Policy Committee. (2010). *'Pentagon Report: Repeal of "Don't Ask, Don't Tell" Can Be Accomplished Successfully, Initiated Immediately.'* [Special report]. https:/./www.dpc. senate.gov/docs/sr-111-2-174.pdf.

155 Democratic Policy Committee. Pentagon Report.

156 Epley, N. (2014). *Mindwise: How We Understand What Others Think, Believe, Feel, and Want.* Knopf.

while doing so.[157] To get to the root of this difference, and the difference in outcomes it could make, Epley and his team of researchers simulated a situation that later played out similarly in real life. In the simulation they created, groups of four people were given the same facts about what it would take to sustain the local fishing industry.

Each group was asked to explore how to solve the dilemma fairly for all stakeholders, including other fishermen, and decide how many fish their group would harvest the following year. The control group were only required to decide the number of fish their group would catch. The other group was asked to take other stakeholder perspectives before deciding on their projected harvest.

The researchers found that perspective-taking exaggerated the perceived differences between the groups, increased distrust and enhanced selfishness. When this simulation was repeated in real life, the end result was that perspective-taking resulted in a more rapid collapse of the fishing ecosystem.[158]

What this research shows is that perspective-taking can cause more problems than solutions. This is worrying because when groups are in conflict, they are often advised to consider the other party's perspective to find a solution without being taught about how to *get* a perspective, versus how to *take* a perspective. This can be exacerbated by the fact that we tend to believe we can accurately take other people's perspectives like it's a sixth sense we can trust. However, that sixth sense has limits.

---

157 Epley, N. (2018). 'Perspective Mistaking: Accurately Understanding the Mind of Another Requires Getting, Not Taking Perspective.' *Journal of Personality and Social Psychology.* https://www.researchgate.net/publication/324232939_Perspective_mistaking_ Accurately_understanding_the_mind_of_another_requires_getting_perspective_not_ taking_perspective#:~:text=A%20final%20experiment%20confirmed%20that,existing%20 knowledge%20about%20another%20person.

158 Epley. Mindwise.

In high-stakes situations, getting perspectives by asking for them is better than taking them and it's far better than using our imagination to walk in someone else's shoes.

When you seek out and listen to people with different perspectives and are deeply curious about the 'why' behind their responses, you will be more confident to lead complex change and find a quicker path to the next eye of the storm.

To be a truly centred leader, you must get curious about people's experiences, values, beliefs and cultural expectations. The depth of insight you gain will also enable you to understand whether you have gained enough mastery to trust in your intuition.

Leadership growth is a lifelong opportunity

As my son approached his 13th birthday, I couldn't understand why he was so excited. He was brimming with anticipation. Curious questioning revealed that he thought becoming a teenager would grant him unprecedented freedom, a magical transformation where he would no longer be subject to parental guidance. Reality delivered a rude awakening.

When he was a teenager, he was less optimistic about the magical transformation that adulthood promised. As a young man he has realised that growth is filled with ups and downs, and that it is quite possibly never-ending. As leaders looking to lead from the centre of the storm, we need to understand this as well.

Robert Kegan's theory about the stages of adult development helps us understand that people's responses in new situations differ based on their development stage.[159] He theorised that adults go through four distinct developmental stages.

The Stages of Adult Development

Stage 1: Self-sovereign (approximately 10-15% of adult population)

Stage 2: Socialised (approximately 45% of the adult population)

Stage 3: Self-authoring (approximately 45% of the adult population)

Stage 4: Self-transforming (perhaps 2% of the adult population)[160]

These stages are not ways of doing but of being in the world.

Leading complex change is challenging but presents many opportunities to continue developing as an adult and a leader. Understanding the stages of adult development will also help you better understand the reactions and responses you see from other people as you lead the change and navigate from one eye of the storm to the next. When you understand the stages, you start to see how people respond to changing situations differently and can begin to anticipate and tailor the support they will need for more effective decision-making and problem-solving.

---

159 Kegan, R. (1982). 'The evolving self: Problem and process in human development.' *Harvard University Press*; Berger, J. (2003). 'A summary of the Constructive-Developmental Theory of Robert Kegan.' https://www.beeleaf.com/wp-content/uploads/2017/09/Kegan-constructive-development-of-adults-narrative.pdf.

160 Garvey-Berger, J. (2013). *Changing on the Job: Developing Leaders for a Complex World.* Stanford University Press.

The self-sovereign mind

In the early stages of development (typically emerging in adolescence), individuals with a self-sovereign mind focus primarily on their own needs and desires. They may struggle with abstract thinking and perspective-taking and this helps explain why we can get exasperated at teenagers and young adults. In terms of leadership, leaders with a self-sovereign mind are primarily motivated by extrinsic rewards and sanctions that are framed by their own self-interest.

The socialised mind

As people progress to develop a socialised mind, they become more influenced by the values and expectations of their culture or immediate social circle. Their responses to new challenges are often guided by the established norms and practices of the people they identify with most closely. They conform to group norms and expectations, and their ability to handle complexity is limited to the frameworks provided by their surrounding social environment. Research results suggest that many adults operate within this stage, making it a common developmental plateau for many.[161] It also helps explain why, as a leader, you also get frustrated when team members seem to follow the crowd and fail to think independently. You may even find yourself doing this at times. In fact, leaders in this stage of adult development are typically very local to the organisation's mission and culture. And they judge success by external standards, such as KPIs, rather than by their own standards and values.

---

161 Garvey-Berger. Changing on the Job.

Self-authoring mind

The next stage is the self-authored mind which is the stage when people develop their own ideologies and frameworks for making sense of the world that are independent of their cultural or social conditioning. This self-authorship allows them to consider various perspectives and create novel solutions to problems, fostering a capacity for greater independence and self-direction. Leaders at this stage know their values and use them, sometimes informed by the perspectives of others, to guide their actions.

Once people reach this stage and begin growing towards the final stage, i.e., a self-transforming mind, we typically see people becoming more comfortable with shades of grey.

Self-transforming mind

Only a very small percentage of people (approximately 2%) <u>fully attain</u> a self-transforming mind. People who reach that stage or who are growing towards it may not only recognise multiple perspectives but also understand the limitations of their own viewpoints. Leaders who are in this stage of development can navigate paradoxes and manage the tension between conflicting ideas, which makes them particularly effective in coming up with innovative solutions to new and unfamiliar challenges that can arise in our changing world.

Understanding your stage of development as an adult and a leader

No matter where you are in the stages of development, when you're under stress, you may temporarily regress to earlier ways of thinking, or find yourself experimenting with more complex ways of understanding that are not yet fully integrated into your way of being.

For instance, if you're a leader transitioning from a predominantly socialised mind towards a self-authored mind you might mostly exhibit behaviours that show a strong influence of external validation and conforming to group norms but occasionally demonstrate moments of independent decision-making and personal authority characteristic of the next stage of development.

Jennifer Garvey-Berger suggests that for people to navigate their growth edges effectively, we need supportive environments that encourage and support us to explore.[162] It's important people are not punished when they put themselves in a vulnerable position and try out new ways of thinking and behaving as they transition to the next stage. It's also important people are not pushed involuntarily towards a growth edge.

But when people are allowed to safely explore the limits of their current stage of adult development and experiment with the new ways of thinking and being that come with the next stage, they are more likely to be able to push through a growth edge.

Please remember that you shouldn't obsess about where you are in the stages. The important takeaways are:

- When you're navigating complex change you must be aware that different people will respond in different ways because of their current form of mind.

- Change is an opportunity to lean into a growth edge – for you and for your team.

If you're a leader frustrated because others rely solely on tried-and-tested responses, understanding the stages will help you remember that those people will benefit from encouragement rather than censure. However, please be cautious about openly labelling people with a specific form of

---

162 Garvey-Berger. Changing on the Job.

mind. Instead, use your curiosity and experiment with different approaches to help you more effectively lead complex change and support other people's development at the same time.

A centred leader recognises and supports other people's growth as they know that is key to successfully navigating complex change. By acknowledging your team members' different stages of development, you can tailor your approach to meet their unique needs and unlock their potential.

Steering the ship through complexity

'In any given moment we have two options: to step forward into growth or to step back into safety.'
Abraham Maslow

The influential American psychologist Abraham Maslow is often quoted as having made this statement. Although he didn't actually say it, it perfectly describes what you need to do as a leader when you step from the eye of the storm out into the storm again.

Leadership is an inside-out journey. A centred leader needs to be able to embrace both emotional and intellectual flexibility – and you can do this by choosing mindfulness, a reflective practice and curiosity, and by fostering growth in yourself and those around you.

By exploring the emotional agility point of your Centring Star, you learn to engage with your own feelings and how those impact how you engage with those around you. You can recognise and work through your emotions with curiosity and kindness allowing you to lead authentically and be present in the moment.

By exploring the intellectual flexibility point of your Centring Star you're able to rethink problems, adopt a beginner's mind and avoid assumptions. You're able to learn to balance your intuition with a willingness to seek and explore different perspectives, stay curious about what's going on around you and in the world and continuously learn and grow.

In the end being a centred leader is not about achieving perfection but about striving for integration. By navigating the inner engagement points of your own Centring Star, you can guide others through the storm and create ripples of positive change that extend far beyond the immediate challenges you face.

But understanding the inner engagement points of your Centring Star is just the first step. Now you have to turn your attention outwards.

PART 5

OUTER ENGAGEMENT

CHAPTER 7

Centring with Contextual Wisdom

When it comes to being a centred leader, we need to focus on our inner world… but that's just the beginning. We also need to learn how to use the outer engagement points of the Centring Star to navigate. But what does this mean?

The outer engagement points of the star

The outer points of the star guide how we interact with the world: connecting with others, navigating social dynamics and influencing our environment. These points reflect the interplay between context and leadership, helping us steer from one complex challenge to the next.

But as we touched on before when you're navigating and leading challenges in a complex world, you'll need to be able to zig and zag, adjusting your course as new information and circumstances unfold. You may miss your original mark, but that isn't necessarily bad. By staying open to possibility and focusing on applying each point of the Centring Star to your journey, you may arrive at a better place, having taken advantage of emerging opportunities along the way.

Confidently leading through complex change requires more than a steady hand. It demands contextual wisdom, inter-relational expertise and tactical agility.

Three wisdoms – personal, people, contextual

Daniel Goleman has written extensively about the importance of emotionally intelligent leaders possessing personal and people wisdom.[163] His model of emotional intelligence describes how self-awareness and self-management enable the exercise of personal wisdom, while social awareness, empathy and social skills are required to enable the exercise of people wisdom.[164] To develop personal and people wisdom you must be able to reflect on past successes and mistakes, so that you know when to act and when to step back.

However, when leading through complex change, you need more than personal and people wisdom. You also need what's known as contextual wisdom. Personal and people wisdom are like a compass that helps you find your direction, but contextual wisdom gives you the map. And without a map, you may not understand the terrain you're navigating.

---

163 Goleman, D. (2006). *Emotional Intelligence: Why It Can Matter More Than IQ*. Bantam.
164 Goleman. Emotional Intelligence.

The Three Wisdoms

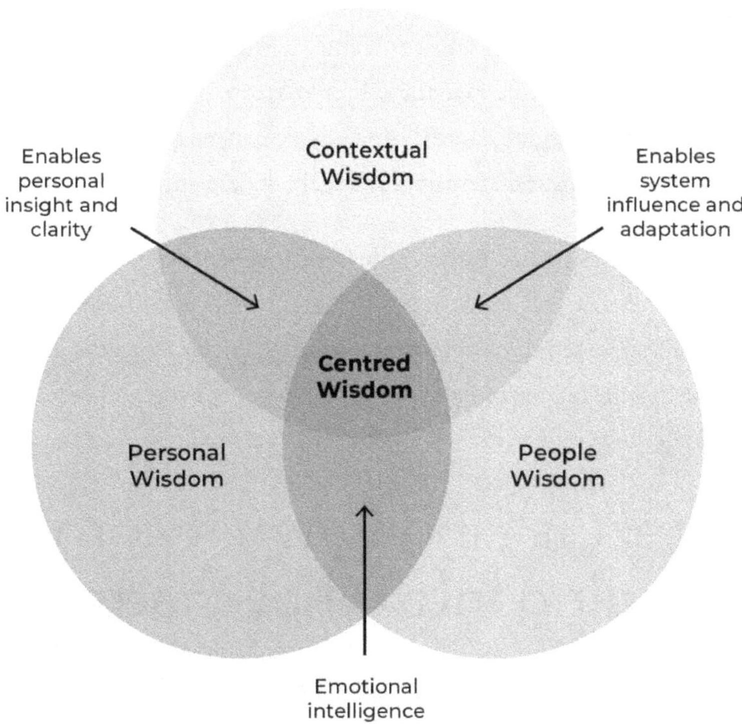

Personal wisdom lets you notice and flexibly manage your emotional state in alignment with your values despite obstacles and setbacks.

People wisdom lets you notice and flexibly respond to the emotional state of others, effectively and sensitively communicate important information and handle any conflicts that may arise.

Contextual wisdom lets you see the bigger picture and recognise patterns others might miss. Where the different wisdoms intersect, we get incredible leadership benefits.

Where personal and people wisdom interact, we get emotional intelligence (much of this we covered in the last two chapters!). Combining contextual and personal wisdom enables us to develop personal insight and clarity as leaders. Where personal and contextual wisdom interact, we create the conditions needed to influence the different actors in the system to change and adapt to the emerging context. And when we have all three wisdoms, we have centred wisdom and are part way to achieving centred leadership.

Each of these are entwined through the Centring Star that guides our centred leadership and lets you empower your team. Of course, throughout your journey you will need to use your values and character strengths as a tether, so you can ensure you remain on the right path – one that is authentically you.

Context is king when it comes to digging into what matters

Today if you're facing the choice between renting a DVD or streaming online, most people would prefer streaming—it's faster, cheaper and more convenient. You can watch whatever you want, whenever and wherever, without the hassle of late fees or scratched discs. (And that's not even considering the very limited rental market available today!)

However, let's revisit the late 2000s. Back then, streaming was still new and unreliable, and physical Blockbuster stores dominated the movie rental market. Netflix, originally a DVD-by-mail service, foresaw the shift in media consumption. Understanding that the context of accessing content was changing, Netflix pivoted to streaming in 2007.[165]

---

165 'How Netflix Moved Operations to the Cloud and Saw Revenue Boom: A Digital Transformation Case Study.' Sharpen. https://sharpencx.com/netflix-digital-transformation-case-study/#:~:text=Netflix%20founders%20Reed%20Hastings%20and,watch%20movies%20and%20consume%20content..

Instead of relying on what they thought they knew, they asked critical questions about customer preferences in the digital age.[166] Because of that Netflix was able to transform its business model to fit the emerging context. This led to significant growth and a revolution in the entertainment industry.

Although Netflix continues to dominate as a streaming service it is not resting on its laurels. It continues to pursue new growth strategies. It pivoted again with the introduction of ad-supported plans targeting people new to Netflix and the more important group of people who cancelled their subscription. At the end of quarter 4, 2023 a massive 40% of new Netflix signups were for the company's ad-supported plan.[167]

By July 2024, Netflix boasted over 277 million subscribers and generated a significant amount of original content rivalling Hollywood studios,[168] while Blockbuster declared bankruptcy in 2010[169] and closed its last corporate store in 2014[170] (though there is still one franchise store open in Bend, Oregon, USA[171]).

---

166 Mier, J & Kohli, A. (17 April 2021). 'Netflix: reinvention across multiple time periods, reflections and directions for future research.' *AMS.* https://doi.org/10.1007/s13162-021-00197-w.

167 Aten, J. (30 January 2024). '1 Number Explains How Netflix Pulled Off the Most Impressive Strategic Shift of All Time—Again.' *Inc.Australia.* https://www.inc-aus.com/jason-aten/1-number-explains-how-netflix-pulled-off-most-impressivestrategic-shift-of-all-time-again.html#:~:text=And%20yet%2C%20in%202007%2C%20Netflix,watch%20and%20stream%20it%20instantly.

168 Singh, S. (9 September 2024). 'Netflix Statistics (Q2, 2024) -- Subscribers & Revenue Data.' Demand Sage. https://www.demandsage.com/netflix-subscribers/.

169 Censky, A. (23 September 2010). 'Blockbuster files for bankruptcy.' CNN Money. https://money.cnn.com/2010/09/23/news/companies/blockbuster_bankruptcy/index.htm.

170 Martin, L. (4 November 2022). 'The True Story of Netflix's Blockbuster, and the Brand's Last Video Rental Store.' *Esquire.* https://www.esquire.com/uk/culture/a41575686/netflix-blockbuster-true-story/.

171 Carmel, J. (6 April 2024). 'A trip to the last Blockbuster on Earth.' *The Washington Post.* https://www.washingtonpost.com/travel/2024/04/06/last-blockbuster-bend-oregon/.

We often hear the phrase 'content is king.' But this suggests that content is more important than context. Bill Gates wrote an essay with that title in 1996, predicting the internet would become a marketplace of information and entertainment.[172] And while his prediction has absolutely come true, we've also found that too much content can be overwhelming and distracting, and it's only valuable if it's relevant and meaningful to the problem at hand. So, when it comes to becoming a centred leader, context, rather than content, is king.

In organisations, contexts you may want to consider include workplace culture, your customers, competitors, industry and even the operating environment.

However, keep in mind the big picture is always bigger than you think it is. One of my former bosses described child safety services as the ambulance waiting at the bottom of the cliff. Everyone was quick to point a finger when something went wrong but slow to look upstream at what was contributing to the problem. Complex challenges like domestic and family violence, drug and alcohol misuse and poor mental health all contributed to children tumbling down the cliff.

In the same way, as a leader, it's crucial to ask questions that go beyond the surface level of what is happening to dig deeper into the context. That is why different elements of the context matter – how other people would perceive the issues and how that affects the situation at hand. Only when you ask questions that go beyond the surface can you get to the heart of the matter. It also means you'll be more likely to notice what's emerging in your specific context and have more time to experiment with and scale up responses that have a positive impact.

---

172 Evans, H. (30 January 2017). '"Content is King" -- Essay by Bill Gates 1996.' *Medium*. https://medium.com/@HeathEvans/content-is-king-essay-by-bill-gates-1996-df74552f80d9.

Mindfulness in context

Exploring your context is closely connected to mindfulness. If you want to find your way into the eye of the storm as a leader surrounded by complexity and ambiguity, you need to get deeply present with what is happening right now (context).

What is emerging from the interactions between different parts of your operating context and beyond? How might you need to respond? What is safe to try? How will you know what impact your actions are having?

Ask yourself the above questions.

You need to think ahead but try not to get ahead of yourself. Get clear about the next few steps and how you will adjust your approach based on what you learn when you step out into the storm again.

Remember, at first the context you can see is only the tip of the iceberg. The captain of the Titanic learnt that the hard way. When you stay in the present and use a beginner's mind, you'll be more likely to stay open to what is emerging and less likely to be caught by the unexpected.

Adopt a systems-thinking approach

When you're trying to figure out your context, it can be like trying to solve a jigsaw puzzle without seeing the full picture. You may connect some pieces by shape or colour, but many pieces remain disconnected or out of place. Adopting a systems-thinking approach will enable you to focus on the whole puzzle and seek to understand how the pieces relate to each other and the bigger picture.

Systems thinking is a holistic approach that examines the interrelationships and interactions within a system, rather than viewing each part in isolation. You will be more likely to see patterns and themes that help organise the pieces into a coherent image and identify gaps and inconsistencies.

The aim should be to identify the leverage points or places where a small change can have a big impact. If the authorising environment doesn't provide the scope to pull the most impactful levers, then influencing and connecting who can is key.

Pictures paint a thousand words

Imagine you are a successful engineer who has been promoted to a management role. You are offered training in technical management skills like budgeting and using the in-house software systems. But you quickly realise these skills are not enough to help you deal with the messy and unpredictable problems that you face as a leader. You need a different approach that helps you understand and respond to the human and social aspects of your organisation and its operating context.

This is what happened to Peter Checkland, one of the pioneers of systems thinking in the 1970s when he faced the reality of leading in an organisation and realised he needed to develop his soft rather than technical skills to be an effective organisational leader.[173] So he developed soft systems methodology (SSM) which enabled him to deal with complex and ill-defined situations.[174]

---

173 Checkland, P. (23 March 2022). 'Systems explained by Peter Checkland.' [Audio]. OpenLearn. https://www.open.edu/openlearn/money-business/leadership-management/systems-explained-peter-checkland.
174 Checkland. Systems explained by Peter Checkland.

SSM recognises that traditional methods don't work well for these types of problems and offers another way to view the situation.

SSM is an often under-utilised means of identifying who you will need to influence as a leader of complex change. A great place to start with SSM is to draw what Checkland calls a rich picture and then interpret it using the pneumonic CATWOE[175].

Your rich picture

The saying 'a picture paints a thousand words' encapsulates the value of a rich picture. As someone trained to write briefs for executive and ministerial decision-makers, I know first-hand how, when you're writing a description of a situation, you're constantly thinking about who the audience is and what they will need and want to know. You're constantly editing and discarding information that doesn't fit the brief.

We tend to do the same when trying to capture and describe complex contexts. However, when we allow ourselves to draw the context (you don't need to be an artist as you're unlikely to share it), we allow our subconscious to begin to make connections and we place our own interpretations on the image that emerges on the paper.

---

175 Checkland, P & Scholes, J. (1990). *Soft Systems Methodology in Action*. John Wiley & Sons.

Using CATWOE

Using the CATWOE pneumonic after drawing a rich picture enables you to develop a succinct problem definition statement.

- **C** = Customers who will receive the benefits or disbenefits of what is being transformed.
- **A** = Actors who will perform the actions to achieve the transformation.
- **T** = Transformations that describe what is changing in the system and what inputs are needed to produce the desired outputs.
- **W** = Worldview statement about what justifies or gives the transformation meaning. This should make sense to a reasonable person you meet on the street.
- **O** = Ownership to describe who controls the system or parts of the system and who could stop or change the transformation.
- **E** = Environmental elements that could influence, limit, or restrict the system's operation. This may include ethical, financial, regulatory or environmental constraints.

This visualisation and interpretation of a complex situation in a rich picture within a pneumonic format captures the main elements, actors, relationships, issues and emotions involved. It helps us explore, clarify and communicate our understanding of the situation and identify opportunities and challenges for improvement.

Rich pictures are particularly useful in situations where multiple stakeholders have different perspectives and priorities. That's because drawing a rich picture allows you to capture the essential elements of a situation, different perspectives and explore the relationships and interactions between them. Remember to see as well as take perspectives.

As Peter Checkland said:

> *'Pictures can be taken in as a whole and help to encourage holistic rather than reductionist thinking about a situation.'*[176]

Ambiguity – your context is overbrimming with it

Back in the 80s, my friend and I had arranged to catch a train into Fortitude Valley, but when the doors closed that night and the train sped off into the night, my friend wasn't in the carriage. I found myself alone on the train, not knowing what had happened to my friend, and there was nothing I could do about it until I could finally get off at our destination station, find a payphone and call their house. That gave me some information – but not a lot. His Dad thought he might be on the next train, but he wasn't sure. So, armed with ambiguous data, I just waited, and eventually, we found each other.

This kind of situation wasn't unusual. There was often no way to get good information once you left your home for the night, but it made me wonder how my kids would cope in a situation where they are stranded without their mobile phones. How would they manage with ambiguous information?

This might seem like it has nothing to do with leadership or work, but a study involving more than 800 people found that people with 'positive attitudes towards ambiguity were more creative, better leaders and better overall performers. They reported lower stress levels and higher incomes than those

---

176 Checkland. Systems explained by Peter Checkland. To learn more about drawing and interpreting a rich picture for your complex work or personal situation, access a free mini-course at www.susanneleboutillier.com/centred/resources.

with negative attitudes towards ambiguity'.[177] And although it found that generations Y and Z expressed as much desire for novel, challenging work as older workers it also found they lacked the skills and confidence required to manage uncertainty when it occurred and were more likely to become anxious.[178]

This finding challenges the common stereotype that because younger people are 'digital natives' they are equipped with the skills required to adapt and innovate. Maybe generational changes in parenting styles (i.e. more 'tiger' and 'helicopter' parents) and technological advances (they can 'Google it' or ask ChatGPT, or an algorithm will just anticipate what they want) are reducing people's exposure to ambiguity. The study suggests that societal changes could have compromised younger generations' ability to manage uncertainty, including bigger, more stress-inducing ambiguities when they do arise.[179] That's why, if you're leading complex change, it's essential to differentiate between an individual's status as a digital native, and their tolerance of ambiguity. They are not the same. If you spent your childhood without access to a smartphone, your tolerance of ambiguity may be different to colleagues who did.

Of course, we can all become conditioned to a different level of ambiguity in context over time. Think back to the stress you experienced the last time your phone battery went flat, or you left it at home, and you desperately wanted to use it to manage some uncertainty in your life. This might have triggered you to feel uncomfortable feelings, or take actions that weren't as tailored as you might otherwise like.

---

177 O'Connor, P & Becker, K. (22 January 2019). 'As work gets more ambiguous, younger generations may be less equipped for it.' *The Conversation*. https://theconversation.com/as-work-gets-more-ambiguous-younger-generations-may-be-less-equipped-for-it-105674.
178 O'Connor. As work gets more ambiguous, younger generations may be less equipped for it.
179 O'Connor. As work gets more ambiguous, younger generations may be less equipped for it.

Determining your ambiguity tolerance

The AdaptiQ Minds Indicator of Ambiguity (I Am) Compass® is a valuable tool for helping you identify why ambiguity is triggering you or members of your team or stakeholders who need to get on board and what you can do to help build a tolerance.[180]

The compass is made up of three dimensions and nine elements as follows:

1. Comfort with ambiguity, i.e., a person's level of ease
   a. Comfort with difficult problems
   b. Comfort with social ambiguity
   c. Comfort with shades of grey
   d. Comfort with unfamiliarity

2. Desire for challenging work, i.e., do they seek it out?
   a. Desire for complexity
   b. Desire for problem solving
   c. Desire for risk taking

3. Managing the uncertainty, i.e., for themselves and those around them.
   a. Managing the lack of clarity
   b. Openness to uncertainty

If you want to lead complex change with confidence, I strongly believe developing your tolerance of ambiguity will go a long way towards ensuring you can maintain high performance and experience less stress, especially if you can support other people around you by managing the uncertainty effectively.

---

180 'The Indicator of Ambiguity (I Am): Embrace Ambiguity.' AdaptiQ Minds. https://adaptiqminds.com/diagnostic-tools/indicator-of-ambiguity/.

So, you think you're assertive?

During a workshop to develop people's capability to embrace the unknown, some participants were extremely surprised to learn that their Indicator of Ambiguity profile identified they should focus on developing the skill 'assertion' to build their tolerance of ambiguity.[181]

I had conversations with several people who were confused because they believed they didn't have a problem with being assertive.

They thought something was wrong with the tool until we started exploring the contexts in which they chose to be assertive and when they didn't. They were very assertive when it came to:

- Protecting the rights of their clients and other staff.
- Asking for resources needed to do their jobs.

However, they did what many intelligent, proactive people with perfectionist tendencies do when things get ambiguous.

They were consistently overprepared and didn't ask for help until they had enough information to feel comfortable to make a decision.

The upside was that they could usually say, *'Here's something I prepared earlier.'* The downside was that they were working much harder than necessary and carrying more of the burden to protect their teams and what they prepared earlier may have a narrow perspective.

You may think that's because they're perfectionists, but it also happens to people who aren't perfectionists.

---

181 'Why is developing a tolerance of ambiguity important?' AdaptiQ Minds. https://adaptiqminds.com/diagnostic-tools/indicator-of-ambiguity/.

It happens because assertive people can fail to be fully assertive in contexts that are ambiguous.

When you accept the inherent unpredictability in an operating environment and adopt a more inclusive stance, you can enable your team and your peers to be more open to exploring new avenues, innovating, and embracing calculated risks.

However, in the face of the unknown, some people tend to withdraw and want to explore the options solo before letting their team or peers know they don't have all the answers. Or they decide to develop and implement plans to cover multiple eventualities because the situation is so uncertain.

Instead, they should assertively seek (rather than take) multiple perspectives. Remember what happened when the ex-military leadership in the United States assumed what would happen if people were allowed to be openly gay in the defence force. Seek other people's perspectives about how the situation could evolve and then assertively establish what needs to be in place for the organisation to respond with agility.

The proverb 'A burden shared is a burden halved' exists because it's a relatable truth and highly relevant when faced with ambiguity. When we share our problems or difficulties with others, they become easier to manage. Get your team to learn from doing and continually adjust the course based on their learning. This will prevent getting stuck in a cycle of overthinking and inaction. Also notice when you are personally holding back and when being more assertive will open up new possibilities.

Being assertive is like having a compass in a storm when faced with ambiguous situations, that are confusing, uncertain, or full of unknowns. It guides you and your team in the right direction while you discard unnecessary cargo and avoid the hidden rocks.

Data lacks meaning without stories

'The key to good decision-making is not knowledge.
It is understanding. We are swimming in the former.
We are desperately lacking in the latter.'
– Malcolm Gladwell[182]

Anyone who has held an executive position would agree that data is important. However, it only provides part of the picture. We must understand that data in context in order to be good (centred) leaders.

When trying to make sense of whether your leadership actions are having the desired impact or determine if you're making progress towards implementing a complex change, it's essential to look beyond what the numbers and other data tell you.

This was made very clear to me when I was leading a transition office that was designed to help separate a single organisation, that at that time had a budget of $10 billion and 80,000 full time equivalent staff, into 17 separate legal entities. The transition office was set up to contribute to the development of responses to national reform negotiations, provide strategic advice and coordinate the portfolio of changes required to implement the reforms and take on the role of lead business change manager.

To complete the transformation, we had over 350 high-level deliverables to undertake across nine work streams. Each stream had its own senior executive accountable for delivery. As the head of the transition office, I was expected to know what was happening and give assurances about what was and wasn't

---

182 Gladwell, M. (2005). *Blink: The power of thinking without thinking.* Little, Brown and Co.

on track and take action to ensure deadlines were met when the need arose. It was easier said than done.

We had all the typical reporting systems in place, but I learned very quickly that people tend to say a project is green and on track when no work has started. How did I learn this? After getting my first nasty surprise at a transition board meeting, I quickly started sending team members out to have coffee or make calls with people involved in the change at all levels of the organisation.

We would then use the stories we heard from those interactions to help us interpret the reports we received before passing them on to the board. If the data and stories didn't seem to match or give the full picture, I would start asking carefully targeted, probing questions to make sense of what was actually going on.

Simple changes to reporting requirements, like requiring people to include a percentage-complete assessment for each deliverable, meant we could assess what work had been completed and what we were hearing from people against deliverable due dates to ascertain if work was genuinely on track. What we were hearing also enabled early identification of risks that could have negatively impacted implementation timelines or the quality of the products delivered. As a result, we were able to provide the board with a more fulsome picture and a comprehensive risk and opportunity assessment.

Data and stories provide different types of information and insights that can help us understand and make sense of what is happening with complex change. Data can help us to identify patterns, trends and relationships within complex systems or phenomena. This can be particularly useful when dealing with large amounts of data or when we need to make comparisons or draw statistical conclusions. However, data alone doesn't always provide us with a full understanding of complex systems or phenomena.

This is where stories come in. Stories, in the form of anecdotes, case studies, narratives and other qualitative accounts, can help us to understand the human and social dimensions of complex change, such as the experiences, beliefs and motivations of individuals and groups involved in those changes.

'Narrative inquiry' is a technique that uses storytelling to explore complex systems. Its developer Dave Snowden argues that stories can capture the complexity and ambiguity of a given situation and reveal the underlying patterns and dynamics that shape it. [183]

Together, data and stories can help us build a more complete and nuanced understanding and identify new questions and areas for further exploration. It makes engaging people's hearts and minds to support change much easier and supports ongoing learning and adaptation, allowing you to adjust your strategies based on real-world feedback. It also prevents you from unnecessarily going down rabbit holes or obsessing over data that, ultimately, is of questionable value.

By combining quantitative and qualitative information, we can gain a more holistic and multidimensional view of the complex systems in which we're operating.

It's like a navigator sailing through unknown waters. The map they're using shows the contours and markers (data). Still, the navigator listens to the tales of local sailors and observes the weather and sea conditions (stories) to make informed decisions before giving advice or acting. Together, the map and the narratives provide the navigator with a comprehensive understanding, ensuring they can more safely and more effectively navigate the unknown waters.

---

183 Kurtz, C & Snowden, D. (2003). 'The new dynamics of strategy: Sense-making in a complex and complicated world.' *IBM Systems Journal.* https://doi.org/10.1147/sj.423.0462.

Chip Heath, a professor of Organisational Behaviour at the Stanford Graduate School of Business, says, 'Data are just summaries of thousands of stories – tell a few of those stories to help make the data meaningful.'[184]

Making more sense of the context

Most people agree the world reached a standstill in March 2020 when the World Health Organisation declared COVID-19 a global pandemic. This announcement was not just a health warning; it set the stage for a multifaceted crisis touching every corner of society. Economic uncertainties soared, public trust in government wavered and health systems were pushed to their limits.

The context of COVID-19 was much broader than just health. While it began with mandates to protect our health, it soon became clear that the interactions between different decisions, health protection measures and various systems had far-reaching implications. The pandemic affected the supply of basic goods and services, leading to shortages of essentials like toilet paper and sanitisers. It also disrupted global supply chains, causing delays and price increases for numerous products.

Schools and universities had to shift to online learning, which highlighted the digital divide and issues of accessibility and equity. The economic impact

---

184 Heath, C & Heath, D. (2007). *Made to Stick: Why Some Ideas Survive and Others Die.* https://edgeservices.bing.com/edgesvc/chat?udsframed=1&form=SHORUN&clientscopes=chat,noheader,udsedgeshop,channelstable,ntpquery,devtoolsapi,udsinwin11,udsdlpconsent,udsfrontload,cspgrd,&shellsig=852f9a01a098258cdabe85a6f-689f081ff7de606&setlang=en-US&lightschemeovr=1&udsps=1&udspp=1https://edgeservices.bing.com/edgesvc/chat?udsframed=1&form=SHORUN&clientscopes=-chat,noheader,udsedgeshop,channelstable,ntpquery,devtoolsapi,udsinwin11,udsdlpconsent,udsfrontload,cspgrd,&shellsig=852f9a01a098258cdabe85a6f689f081ff7de606&setlang=en-US&lightschemeovr=1&udsps=1&udspp=1 Random House.

was profound, with many businesses closing, unemployment rates soaring, and governments implementing unprecedented financial aid packages. Social interactions were also altered, as lockdowns and social distancing measures affected mental health and well-being, leading to increased feelings of isolation and anxiety. Overall, COVID-19 illustrated how interconnected our world is and how decisions in one area can ripple across various aspects of society.

Originally developed as a sense-making tool, the Cynefin (pronounced "kuh-NEV-in") Framework[185], which has been evolving for over 10 years, suddenly became a crucial tool for managing a crisis that defied all norms.[186]

Cynefin comes from the Welsh language and has a deep meaning. It's often translated as 'habitat' or 'place'. But more than a physical location, Cynefin describes a sense of belonging to a particular environment where everything feels right and welcoming. It suggests a natural fit, not just with the physical aspects of a place but also how well it aligns with personal or community identity. This concept is especially useful when talking about how people fit into complex social and environmental systems. It helps us understand our relationship with the world around us.

At its core, Cynefin is a decision-support framework that recognises complexity theory. The creator of the Framework, Dave Snowden, has significantly contributed to the field of knowledge management and the application of complexity science, holds academic positions as an extraordinary professor at several universities and is a respected speaker and author on complexity.

---

185 Snowden, D & Boone, M. (2007). 'A Leader's Framework for Decision Making.' *Harvard Business Review.* https://hbr.org/2007/11/a-leaders-framework-for-decision-making.

186 Kruger, J & Lavarias, R. (23 February 2022). 'Application of the Cynefin Framework to COVID-19 pandemic.' Domestic Preparedness. https://domesticpreparedness.com/public-health/application-of-the-cynefin-framework-to-covid-19-pandemic.

During the pandemic, leaders found themselves grappling with issues ranging from straightforward, such as directing staff to wear personal protective equipment (PPE), to highly complex, like sourcing PPE when demand outstripped supply, and managing public resistance and misinformation. The framework provided a way to classify these challenges and respond with strategies tailored to the nature of the problems they faced.[187]

The framework helped clarify these transitions, enabling leaders to effectively prioritise resources and communications. As the virus evolved and public sentiments fluctuated, the complex and chaotic aspects of the crisis came to the forefront. Here, the Cynefin Framework proved invaluable by helping leaders identify patterns and adapt their strategies to a rapidly-changing environment.

The Cynefin Framework was used to help categorise pandemic-related issues into its five domains—simple, complicated, complex, chaotic and disorder – allowing leaders to tailor their responses to issues as they were identified and categorised.[188]

For instance, during the early stages of the pandemic, many situations fell into the chaotic domain, where immediate, decisive action was necessary to establish order and prevent widespread disaster. As understanding of the virus improved, responses could be adjusted into the complex or even complicated domains, where evidence-based strategies and expert knowledge could guide more structured responses.

Amid overlapping crises, including economic downturns and severe weather events, the framework's role extended beyond the immediate response to the pandemic. Emergency management professionals used it to grasp the multifaceted nature of the crisis. By applying the Cynefin Framework, they could keep pace with the evolving situation, ensuring that their actions were both timely and appropriate.

---

187 Kruger. Application of the Cynefin Framework to COVID-19 pandemic.
188 Kruger. Application of the Cynefin Framework to COVID-19 pandemic.

The Cynefin Framework is not just limited to COVID-19 challenges. It works well for leaders who are leading in any time of complex change. It emphasises the importance of situational awareness and the ability to adapt strategies as situations evolve, which is crucial for tactical agility.

For centred leaders, this means maintaining an awareness of the shifting dynamics within each domain and adjusting your leadership approach accordingly. By understanding that different situations require different responses – ranging from highly structured approaches in the simple domain to adaptive, emergent strategies in the complex domain – leaders can avoid the pitfalls of one-size-fits-all solutions and respond more effectively to dynamic challenges.

The Cynefin Framework – 2020 version[189]

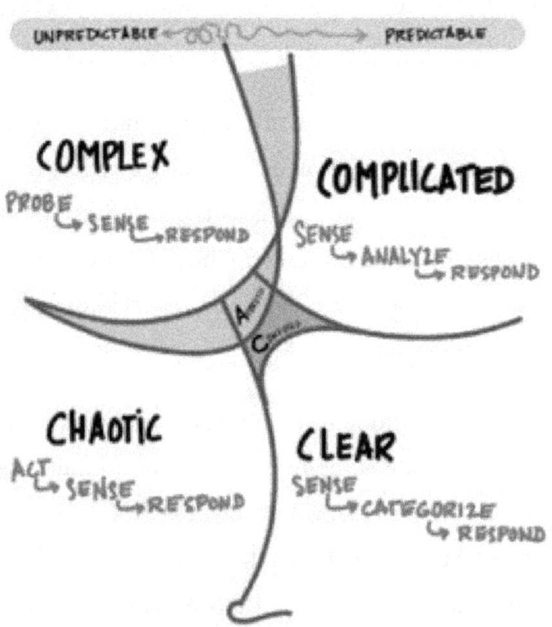

---

189 Snowden, D & Friends. (Riva Greenbert and Boudewijn Bertsch, Eds.) (2021). *Cynefin weaving sense-making into the fabric of our world*. Cognitive Edge Pte Ltd.

The five domains within the framework are:

1. **Simple (Obvious):** This domain involves clear cause-and-effect relationships, where the right answer is self-evident. Decisions are straightforward and based on best practices.

2. **Complicated:** In this domain, cause-and-effect relationships exist but are not immediately apparent. These require expertise and analysis to solve through good practices.

3. **Complex:** Here, cause and effect can only be perceived in retrospect. There are no right answers, so leaders must probe first, then sense and respond. This domain calls for emergent practices.

4. **Chaotic:** In chaotic contexts, there is no clear relationship between cause and effect at the systems level. Leaders must act first to establish order, sense where stability lies and respond to turn the chaotic into the complex.

5. **Disorder:** This domain is used when it is unclear which of the other four domains apply. Leaders need to break down the situation to determine which domain they are truly in.

As a first step, you need to determine where you are in the Framework. For example, in the COVID-19 scenario the lack of clear, consistent social distancing guidelines initially led to chaotic situations. Over time, as more information became available about virus transmission, the response shifted to the complex domain, where leaders used emerging patterns to adapt guidelines and improve public compliance and safety measures.

As leaders we might see this instead when a significant deliverable will not be achieved on time, but there are many moving parts and it's not clear which link in the chain is causing the problem. At first it may seem like an overwhelming number of elements could be causing the problem but by using the Cynefin Framework and categorising each link in the chain you can more easily identify how each of those links needs to be managed to achieve the deliverable.

Exploring which domain most applies to your events and issues is only the beginning. Next, you need to make sense of the situation. We've already covered how you can use a combination of data and stories to reveal patterns and insights. You can also use probes, which are small, safe-to-fail experiments designed to test hypotheses and explore the complexities of a situation. These probes help you gather additional insights. You can also look for weak signals of emerging changes or shifts within the system.

After you've made initial sense of the situation (remember it will continue to evolve) you need to learn what is possible. However, we can only truly understand what is possible in complex systems when we take multiple actions simultaneously. This avoids the initial success bias of new actions and ensures a wide range of potential outcomes. Before you take action, you also need to think through how you are going to capture feedback about the impact of your actions on the system, so you can interpret that information, adjust your responses and keep heading in the desired direction.

When using the Cynefin Framework for centred leadership, you should keep in mind:

- It is a sense-making device to categorise problems so you can apply the right leadership style and response.
- Avoid using it as a rigid categorisation tool because misapplying the framework, such as forcing a complex problem into a simple solution, can lead to inappropriate strategies.

There is a lot more to using Cynefin than I have described here. However, it's such an enormously valuable tool that I could not write a book about being a centred leader without identifying it as one of the critical tools you should be using.

Dave Snowden, world-leading researcher on leading through complexity, compares leading complex change to being a sculptor who creates new shapes and patterns by moving a magnet over a table filled with iron filings.[190] Each motion of the magnet organises the filings into unique formations, influenced by the magnet's strength, its proximity and the initial spread of the filings.[191]

This process mirrors how centred leaders can utilise the Cynefin Framework to work out their next right step out of the eye of the storm as they lead complex change. The Framework will help you discern the emerging patterns, enabling you to tailor your strategies to the nuances of each specific situation.

When context is king, your responses must keep evolving to keep pace with the emerging context.

---

190 Göthe, M. (16 August 2022). 'Interview with Dave Snowden about Leading Complexity.' crisp. https://blog.crisp.se/2022/08/16/michaelgothe/interview-with-dave-snowden-about-leading-complexity.
191 Göthe. Interview with Dave Snowden about Leading Complexity.

Choosing how to show up

A trip to MONA (Museum of Old and New Art) in Tasmania had me reflecting on the value of how we choose to show up when change is full of confusing information, an abundance of uncertainty and many unknowns.

MONA is a unique and unconventional museum that showcases contemporary art from around the world. Before you arrive, you are instructed to download an app that allows you to explore the museum at your own pace and discover more about each artwork that interests you.

When I arrived at MONA, I was excited and curious. I noticed a long line of people in front of the elevator going down into the museum and another line of people choosing to go down the stairwell beside the elevator. There were no clear instructions, so I joined the people on the stairs, exited the next level down, and started exploring the different exhibits.

As I wandered around, I was amazed by the variety and creativity of the artworks. Some were beautiful, some were disturbing, some were interactive and some were hidden. I felt like I was on a treasure hunt, never knowing what I would find next.

As I immersed myself in the different experiences, I couldn't always figure out how to get from one level to the next. However, sometimes I was assertive and asked a nearby MONA team member how to navigate. At other times, I backtracked but discovered something new and interesting on my way down.

Only when I got to the lowest level and almost all the way through did I realise the intent was to catch the lift to the bottom floor and work your way up. I've since reflected on whether this twist brought about by ambiguity detracted from my MONA experience. It didn't, and I was curious about why.

Then I remembered that it comes down to how you choose to show up. I chose to show up with curiosity, openness and a belief I could find my way through the maze that is MONA. I consciously embraced the uncertainty, relished the journey and let others know when I needed support. I chose to view the ambiguity as a gateway to new knowledge and experiences rather than a hurdle to overcome.

This reminded me of the research of Martin Seligman, the founder of positive psychology and a member of the research team that discovered 'learned helplessness'.[192] This early discovery led him to study resilience and how people thrive despite struggle. His research found that one key factor contributing to our resilience is how we explain the events that happen to us.[193]

Seligman says, 'While you can't control your experiences, you can control your explanations.'[194]

Resilient people tend to explain negative events as temporary, specific and external rather than permanent, global and internal.

Imagine you spill milk all over the floor. Instead of thinking, 'I'm such a klutz; I'll never get anything right,' a resilient person would say, 'That was clumsy of me, but it's just a bit of milk, and it'll be cleaned up in no time.'

Or if you're faced with a challenging situation, you might say, 'This is a difficult situation, but it will pass' rather than 'This is hopeless and will never change.' It's like looking at a cloudy sky and thinking, 'Well, it's going to be sunny eventually,' rather than, 'Looks like I'm living under a permanent rain cloud now.'

192 Seligman, M. (2011). 'Building Resilience.' *Harvard Business Review.* https://hbr.
     org/2011/04/building-resilience.
193 Seligman. Building Resilience.
194 Seligman. Building Resilience.

And, if something happens you have no control over, you might say, 'This is due to factors outside my control, but I can still do something about it,' rather than, 'This is my fault, and I can't do anything about it.'

By adopting a more resilient explanatory style, we can cope better with ambiguity and uncertainty and see them as opportunities for learning and growth rather than threats and obstacles. We can also cultivate a more positive outlook and attitude that enables us to boost our well-being and performance.

CHAPTER 8

Centring with Inter-relational Expertise

In previous chapters we covered self-awareness (knowing what you're feeling and why you're feeling it), self-management (how you effectively handle distressing and positive emotions) and contextual wisdom (seeing things in context for more insight). Now we need to talk about interpersonal expertise or 'people wisdom'.

As we've seen previously, people wisdom – or what we might call interpersonal expertise – is part of how we engage externally and guides us to our centred leadership. This is essentially the ability to communicate, and build and navigate relationships with others. And it's vital to leadership because it's how we inspire, motivate and engage our teams, particularly during times of chaos and change.

Applying the outer engagement points of the star

In chapter 7 we introduced and explored the concept of outer engagement i.e. the points of the Centring Star, which consists of contextual wisdom, inter-relational expertise and tactical agility. In this chapter we will delve deeper into this idea of inter-relational expertise and discover how it forms a crucial point of the Centring Star needed to guide you as a centred leader. By applying all outer engagement points of the star to your journey, you develop the capacity to navigate the complex challenges and interactions that arise when leading through complex change.

Starting with emotional intelligence

But to understand interpersonal expertise we need to understand the broad framework of emotional intelligence as developed by Daniel Goleman, which arises at the intersection of personal and people wisdom, sometimes referred to as competence.[195]

---

195 Goleman, D. (2006). *Emotional Intelligence: Why It Can Matter More Than IQ.* Bloomsbury Publishing.

Daniel Goleman's Model of Emotional Intelligence[196] (adapted)

	Recognition	Regulation
Personal Wisdom	**Self-Awareness** • Self-confidence • Awareness of your emotional state • Recognising how your behaviour impacts others • Paying attention to how others influence your emotional state	**Self-Management** • Keeping disruptive emotions and impulses in check • Acting in congruence with your values • Handling change flexibly • Pursuing goals and opportunities despite obstacles and setbacks
People Wisdom	**Social Awareness** • Picking up on the mood in the room • Caring what others are going through • Hearing what the other person is "really" saying	**Relationship Management** • Getting along with others • Handling conflict effectively • Clearly expressing ideas/information • Using sensitivity to another person's feeling (empathy) to manage interactions successfully

Goleman's matrix describes how self-awareness and self-management enable the exercise of personal wisdom, while social awareness, empathy and social skills are required to enable the exercise of people wisdom, or inter-relational expertise. Interpersonal expertise entails the development of social competence, which encompasses social awareness and relationship management.

---

196 Axiak, Rosalba. (2023). The Pain Within-Full Thesis. 10.13140/RG.2.2.24419.43045.

Social awareness involves understanding others' emotions, empathising with them and genuinely listening. This skill set includes sensing people's feelings, grasping their unique viewpoints and taking an active interest in their concerns. It also involves having a keen sense of organisational awareness and a strong service orientation.

Relationship management, on the other hand, focuses on effectively getting along with others, resolving conflicts, clearly expressing ideas and managing others' emotions with sensitivity. It requires teamwork and collaboration, the ability to inspire and lead and the skill to settle disagreements constructively.

Personal wisdom is like using a GPS on a solo trip. You're only focused on your own direction and progress. But navigating complex change as a centred leader is more like going on a road trip with friends. You need to know where you're headed and how to make sure everyone's comfortable, engaged and contributing to the journey. And you need to inspire them to do this while staying clear of the ravages of the storms all around you.

So while social awareness helps you read the group dynamics, relationship management ensures the trip doesn't derail due to conflicts or miscommunication. And both of them together lead to the inter-relational expertise you need for your centred leadership journey.

In his book *Social Intelligence: The New Science of Human Relationships*, Goleman says, 'When we focus on others, our world expands'.[197]

When it comes to inter-relational expertise, I believe that when we as leaders focus on others, our possibilities expand!

---

197 Goleman. D. (2007). *Social Intelligence: The New Science of Human Relationships.* Arrow Ltd – Mass Market.

Competition as a catalyst for centred leaders

I have always loved swimming. When I was a kid, I joined the local swimming club and competed in various events. I wasn't the fastest swimmer, and I was happy when I won a bronze medal. But every year, I trained hard to win a points trophy because that meant I was constantly improving my personal best. I didn't care much about beating others, I just wanted to beat myself.

One of my childhood friends was very different. She liked to win, no matter what. And this is something that hasn't changed over the years. On a holiday cruise she was in a friendly competition with other guests to win a very special prize – a cruise line key ring.

She did everything she could to win that key ring, including laying on top of and rolling over another male passenger she didn't know to secure the win. The key ring ended up in the bin, but she will always treasure the memory of winning the competition.

Luckily, as a senior leader in her organisation, she can separate her desire to win outside work from her behaviour as a leader at work. As a leader, she has inter-relational expertise, and understands people, knowing when to collaborate and when to compete. A part of being a centred leader is knowing how to use competition as a catalyst for good on your journey to centred leadership.

How does that work? Well, we all know that competition can be detrimental to you and your workplace culture, but it can also be a catalyst for innovation and performance. We're talking about competition here, because it's an integral part of life, a force that can propel us forward, challenge us and foster growth. And because it's an integral part of life, it's also something that you need to understand as part of inter-relational expertise. When we understand our own relationship with competition, we can recognise when it manifests in healthy or unhealthy ways.

This self-awareness is the first step towards harnessing the power of competition for your personal leadership growth and well-being, and for understanding how it could be harnessed to increase your inter-relational expertise. When you challenge yourself or others in a positive, productive and respectful manner, you are engaging in healthy competition. You celebrate your achievements and learn from your failures. You recognise the strengths and contributions of others, and you cooperate when needed. You enjoy the process of competing, not just the outcome.

On the other hand, unhealthy competition is when you compete with yourself or others in a disrespectful, unfair and destructive way. You focus on beating others and proving yourself superior. You feel threatened by others' success and sabotage or undermine them. You are obsessed with winning, and you can't handle losing. You ignore the rules, ethics, and consequences of your actions.

The reality is that many workplaces are highly competitive – and not always in a way that's conducive to healthy growth. However, Netherlands researchers Kyriaki Fousiani and Barbara Wisse found that leaders in highly competitive work environments who view their power as a responsibility rather than a personal opportunity have more positive and higher-quality leader-follower relationships.[198] Those relationships provide an opportunity to positively influence the culture of competition in the workplace.

---

198 Fousiani, K & Wisse, B. (31 January 2022). 'Effects on Leaders' Power Construal on Leader-Member Exchange: The Moderating Role of Competitive Climate at Work.' Midwest Academy of Management. https://journals.sagepub.com/doi/full/10.1177/15480518221075229.

If you think of competition as a spice, you'll know that a little bit of spice can enhance the flavour of your dish, but too much spice can ruin it. You don't want to add spice to everything you cook, and you don't want to use the same spice for every recipe. You want to choose the right spice for the right occasion and use it in moderation. Similarly, you don't want to compete in everything you do, and you don't want to use the same competitive style for every situation. You want to choose the right type of competition for the right goal and use it in balance. When you play with competition as part of your inter-relational expertise you need to find what fits best for you, your organisation and your future as a centred leader.

I will leave you to ponder these wise words from Brian Herbert, author of the *Dune* series:

'In every competition, there are no winners or losers, only learners.'

The power of generative dialogue

In a non-government organisation that was busily responding to the needs of clients living with a mix of complex vulnerabilities, the executive team struggled with endless leadership discussions about an ongoing challenge that led nowhere. They cared deeply about their work and many projects, but each person's strong attachment to their own ideas caused friction. Then, their Chief Executive brought me in and introduced the concept of generative dialogue.

The Theory of Generative Dialogue (also known as The Four Fields of Conversation) was introduced by Otto Scharmer, senior lecturer at MIT. It's designed to highlight conversational patterns that people need to navigate through every day. To do that it sets out fields of dialogue that include:

1. Talking nice
2. Talking tough
3. Reflective dialogue
4. Generative dialogue[199]

Generative dialogue is the final space we want to strive to bring our conversations into – the ultimate goal in dialogue – because it's here that we're now 'more interested in serving larger or deeper creative processes with our senses and listening.'[200]

When the CEO brought generative dialogue into the picture it allowed the team to use a structured process so they could break old patterns, consciously set aside judgements and truly listen to each other. And when they did, the team then started building on each other's ideas and feelings. This shift from endlessly circling discussions to gaining clarity and laying out a direction together sparked new innovations and a renewed spirit of teamwork.

As a facilitator, I've learned to avoid the word 'discussion' whenever possible and use 'quality conversation' instead. This is because when you look up the definition of 'discuss' you realise it refers to debating a topic, in other words, trying to convince the other person that you are right or shattering and breaking something into pieces. It also means to examine or search thoroughly. Still, the other definitions have such negative connotations when demonstrating interpersonal expertise that it doesn't sound like that exploration would be a pleasant process.

---

199 Flaherty, S. (April 2016). 'The Journey to Creating Our Circle of Six: Exploration of Otto Scharmer's Four Fields of Conversation.' University of Massachusetts Boston. http://www. cct.umb.edu/files/SFlaherty-RPPexample-2017Feb13.pdf.

200 Flaherty. The Journey to Creating Our Circle of Six.

Conversations can lose focus without good facilitation and participants may find it hard to set aside their biases. However, I'm not suggesting you bring in an external facilitator for every conversation, but you do need to consider how you frame and manage the quality of the conversation.

When we enter into a dialogue, we listen without parameters or a pre-determined sense of what's reasonable and what is not. Daniel Kahneman identified two systems of thinking. System 1 where we think fast like we're on auto-pilot, relying on what we already know to guide our actions, or system 2 where our thinking is slower, more considered and open to noticing differences and nuances. This second type of thinking is the type we need to do when we enter a dialogue.[201]

When we embrace slow thinking we turn off established patterns and bring a beginner's mind to the conversation. We get curious, we're aware of what we're noticing, and we consider what our reactions might mean. Essentially, we go below the surface and explore that part of the iceberg hiding under the waves.

For quality conversations we also need to embrace listening. Leadership development consultants and researchers Jack Zenger and Joseph Folkman found that people perceived as the most effective listeners do more than just passively listen.[202] The most effective listeners engage in a dialogue where the listener acts like a trampoline. They bounce rather than absorb ideas and energy. They amplify those ideas, building the other person's energy and clarity of thinking.

---

201 Kahneman, D. (2011). *Thinking, Fast and Slow.* Farrar, Straus and Giroux; Kannengiesser, U & Gero, J. (22 May 2019). 'Design thinking, fast and slow: A framework for Kahneman's dual-system theory in design.' Cambridge University Press. https://www.cambridge.org/core/journals/design-science/article/design-thinking-fast-and-slow-a-framework-for-kahnemans-dualsystem-theory-in-design/A200DC637BBDC982D288FC4F8A112DE7.

202 Zenger, J & Folkman, J. (15 July 2016). 'What Great Listeners Actually Do?' *Harvard Business Review.* https://hbr.org/2016/07/what-great-listeners-actually-do.

Lynda Gratton and Sumantra Ghoshal mapped the different types of conversations we have across four quadrants:[203]

Map of Conversations

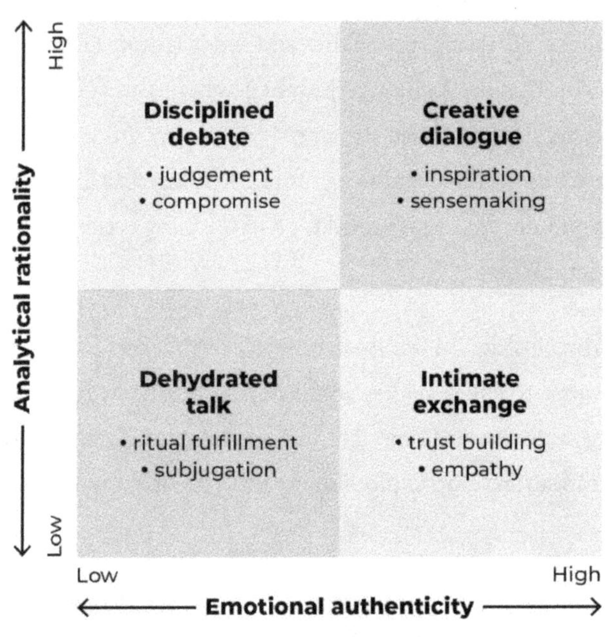

Gratton and Ghoshal, 2002

When determining where you are on the four quadrants, ask yourself:

- Where on the map is the bulk of my conversation?

- Are my conversations where I want them to be?

- Does my team follow the same rules and end up debating everything discussed?

---

203 Gratton, L & Ghoshal, S. (2002). 'Improving the quality of conversations.' *Organizational Dynamics*. https://www.researchgate.net/publication/256923944_Improving_the_Quality_of_Conversations.

Disciplined debate might be appropriate at times, for example when checking compliance requirements. However, it can stifle creativity when exploring a complex issue or a possible innovation.

Talk may be dehydrated if people feel it is pointless sharing their ideas or feelings when meeting agendas do not allow sufficient time for genuine dialogue. People could be afraid of sharing their feelings if conversations are overly facts-based, and emotion is discouraged.

Creative dialogue happens when thinking and feeling come together in creative, insightful and energising conversations. This is precisely what is needed when a team or group of stakeholders has to lead complex change. And you certainly need it if you want to keep centred as a leader. Negative conversations (negative in approach rather than in topic) can push you further away from a storm eye and cause you to get lost in the chaos of the storm.

Of course, finding that conversation sweet spot takes effort and a willingness to experiment. No one wants to spend their time in dehydrated conversations, but the other conversations on the map all have a place. The trick is to create the conditions for the right kind of exchange for the context.

Rationality and emotions both have a place in your quality conversations

If rationality is about using a structured approach to find an answer to your problem, emotions are about finding meaning because quality conversations are about more than thoughts. They combine both ideas and feelings to create meaning so you and others can make sense of a situation. It's similar to why data and stories are so valuable when combined – it brings the rational and emotional aspects together to provide a balanced picture.

When someone suggests a course of action, confidently ask your team how they feel about it. Dig deeper and ask why, if it's not clear at first. Doing so will either generate a commitment to the action or identify issues that must be explored before deciding on a course of action. An action may make rational sense on the surface, but ethical concerns may come to the fore if people (team members or stakeholders) share why the idea makes them feel uncomfortable. It could also identify the need for you to improve how you support your team or stakeholders to manage any uncertainties.

I hope you see the value in enabling generative dialogue rather than traditional discussions, especially when learning to navigate according to your Centring Star. Dialogue that generates ideas and action encourages exploration, builds shared understanding and emphasises active listening, all of which foster creativity, collaboration and innovation.

Think of generative dialogue as a bridge connecting two shores. Each shore represents a different idea or opinion. Without a bridge, the shores remain isolated, making communication and collaboration difficult. But a strong bridge – effective dialogue – connects these shores, allowing ideas to flow, build upon each other and create a shared path toward common goals.[204]

Creating a safe space for generative dialogue often takes time, trust or someone who can challenge people with sensitivity to create a safe space for this kind of conversation. However, it's worth creating that space as Gratton and Ghoshal found that the most energising and creative conversations occur when rationality and emotions are combined.[205] Creating a safe space for open conversation is also key to effecting complex change. William Isaacs, former senior lecturer at MIT Sloan School of Management and an expert

---

204 Kline, N. (1999). *Time to Think: Listening to Ignite the Human Mind.* Octopus Publishing Group; Havers, E. (2008). 'A study of whether, and how meetings held in a Thinking Environment impact organisational life.' [Research thesis.] https://www.timetothink.com/wp-content/uploads/2019/10/booklet_a5_download_1.pdf.
205 Gratton. Improving the quality of conversations.

in dialogue and conversation, talks about how generative dialogue brings parties to new understanding and coordinated action by learning the art of thinking together, again essential for leading complex changes.[206]

To create a safe space, we also need to make sure that people feel psychologically safe. In her book *The Fearless Organization: Creating Psychological Safety in the Workplace for Learning, Innovation and Growth*, Amy Edmondson explains how Google's Project Aristotle highlighted the critical role of psychological safety in unleashing the power of smart people in teams.[207]

The Project Aristotle researchers found that psychological safety was the most important factor contributing to high performance even though the teams in the research study also had clear goals, colleagues they could depend on and work they found meaningful and impactful.[208]

Amy Edmondson's research found that when you exhibit the following leadership behaviours, you'll create a space that cultivates psychological safety.

1. **Be accessible and approachable** so everyone can be involved in learning together.

2. **Acknowledge the limits of your current knowledge** so other people feel comfortable to do the same.

3. Willingly but **authentically display fallibility** so people understand you tolerate failure.

4. Engage people and encourage them to be responsive by **inviting participation from others** before you have the answers.

---

206 Isaacs, W. (1999). *Dialogue: The art of thinking together.* Currency.
207 Edmondson, A. (2018). *The fearless organization: Creating psychological safety in the workplace for learning, innovation, and growth.* John Wiley & Sons.
208 Edmondson. The fearless organization.

5. Use **failures as learning opportunities** so people can productively deal with failure.

6. Use direct, actionable language to **encourage frank conversations** that enable people to learn.

7. Help people feel more psychologically safe by **setting clear, consistent boundaries**.

8. **Hold people to account in a fair and consistent way** when people stray across boundaries.[209]

Inter-relational expertise is key to getting your team to embrace decisions

Do you remember the classic video about the first follower – the one set at a music festival where a lone person is dancing until first one person and then others are brave enough to follow them?[210] You can be the most centred leader in relation to understanding the context and knowing when to change tactics but when you are a leader, you are not alone. You need people to follow you to achieve sustainable or adaptable change. And that means people need to embrace decisions otherwise actions designed to implement change will be doomed to failure.

Decision buy-in happens when people understand and accept why decisions are made. You could send out a memo (one-way communication) or you

---

209 Edmondson, A. C. (2012). Teaming: How organizations learn, innovate, and compete in the knowledge economy. Jossey-Bass.

210 nanoKnowledge. (5 October 2014). *Pioneering Leadership: First Follower Principle.* [Video]. YouTube. https://www.youtube.com/watch?v=3EKAxQbYA9U.

could engage key people in a conversation – we've already explored the value of a quality two-way dialogue.

However, what if your team or stakeholders have repetitive conversations that don't result in an outcome? Are they really quality conversations? Or do you suspect important perspectives are missing in action? I've worked with clients who feel the same way.

They have team and stakeholder meetings about critical issues where a few dominant voices take centre stage while others remain silent. Implementing a structured decision-making process, where each person is allowed to share their thoughts and opinions, regardless of personality type, enables the surfacing of a range of perspectives, a more nuanced conversation and, not surprisingly, a more-informed decision. Using a structured process ensures everyone's voice is heard and facilitates conversation participant understanding of why a specific course of action is chosen or discarded. This in turn increases the degree to which decisions are not only accepted but supported.

Nancy Kline is an influential author and leadership coach known for her work on creating environments that foster clear and independent thinking in organisations. Her key concept, the 'Thinking Environment,' is based on the idea that the quality of everything we do depends on the quality of our thinking first.[211] Kline suggests that people produce their best ideas when they feel genuinely respected and free to think for themselves. But to create this space as centred leaders, we have to tap into our inter-relational expertise, focusing on others around us, where they are and what they need.

We've already touched on Amy Edmondson's work on creating psychologically safe spaces which allows people to speak up, share information and ask

---

211 Kline, N. (1999). *Time to Think: Listening to Ignite the Human Mind.* Octopus Publishing Group.

important questions when it matters.[212] Although Nancy Kline's work is also about creating spaces that are essentially also psychologically safe, the driver for doing so is broader than enabling safety. In this case it's to improve the quality of people's thinking, their ability to contribute their thoughts to improve the overall quality of a group's thinking, decision inputs and acceptance of those resulting decisions.

Inspiring people to embrace decision making is crucial if you don't want to lose people in the turbulence of the storm.

A Thinking Environment comprises 10 components, each designed to support better thinking.[213] These include:

1. **Attention:** Listen respectfully and genuinely without interrupting. For example, during a team meeting, let each person speak without cutting them off, showing their input is valued.

2. **Incisive questions:** Ask questions that challenge assumptions and open new ideas. For example, in a brainstorming session, ask, 'What are we assuming about our customers that might not be true?'

3. **Equality:** Treat everyone as equal partners in thinking, giving everyone a chance to contribute. For example, in a project review, ensure junior and senior team members have equal time to share their perspectives.

4. **Appreciation:** Genuinely acknowledge positive qualities and efforts, aiming for a ratio of five praises for every criticism (remember Barbara Frederickson's research on positive emotional attractors (PEAs)?). For example, when giving feedback, say, 'Your detailed report really helped us understand the issues. It would

---

212 Edmondson. The fearless organization.
213 'The Ten Components.' Time To Think. https://www.timetothink.com/thinking-environment/the-ten-components/.

be good to see all the points you raised clearly summarised in the conclusion.'

5. **Ease:** Create a calm environment where people don't feel rushed. For example, in a strategy meeting, allocate enough time to talk about issues so team members can think clearly without pressure.

6. **Encouragement:** Foster a culture of mutual support rather than competition. For example, celebrate team achievements and encourage collaboration over individual competition.

7. **Feelings:** Allow people to express their true feelings, believing it leads to better thinking. For example, in a performance review, ask, 'How do you feel about your workload?' and listen to their concerns.

8. **Information:** Ensure a steady flow of accurate information and keep everyone informed. For example, regularly share updates during team stand-ups so everyone knows the current status and next steps.

9. **Place:** Design a physical space that shows people they matter. For example, arrange comfortable meeting rooms with the necessary resources so everyone feels valued and welcome. This could include ensuring the inclusion of important cultural symbols such as flags or artwork associated with First Nations peoples.

10. **Diversity:** Value different perspectives and identities within the team. For example, in project planning, actively seek input from team members with varied backgrounds to enrich the ideas and solutions.

Understanding and using these components can benefit leaders who are managing complex changes and volatile situations because thinking environments facilitate deeper insight, innovation and commitment to shared goals. When people feel safer and more valued, they're encouraged to share their thoughts and ideas openly. And when people believe their contributions matter, they are more likely to engage meaningfully with challenging issues and support sustainable changes.

For leaders aiming to implement these principles, the key is to consistently apply the components of a Thinking Environment in daily interactions and structured meetings. Remember, making a good decision is about more than the outcome. It's also about the process and how team members perceive it.

Curiosity drives connection

Early in my career, I often sat on one side of the table, supporting senior managers in implementing change while union officials and delegates, concerned about how the change would affect them, sat on the other. It wasn't unusual for the union officials to get worked up and put on a show for their members. Many managers found it hard not to take the union slurs personally.

After one particularly heated meeting, I received a call from a manager asking me how I managed to have a friendly, personal conversation with the union official after the meeting. The answer was simple. I needed to. Because building and maintaining a rapport with union officials was essential for me to do my job well.

I was able to do this because I learnt to play the issue, not the person. However, I also learnt not to ignore the person. And as a centred leader, this is a part of inter-relationships that you must embrace as well.

Working with stakeholders at an inter-jurisdictional level, I saw many bureaucrats fall into the trap of failing to connect with stakeholders and then wonder why they faced so many barriers to effecting change. Forming a deeper, personal connection with stakeholders in such situations can be awkward. Our instinct to stand back and protect ourselves is natural. Not only is the situation socially ambiguous, but how they see you is also coloured by whether they're getting what they want. And that is exactly why you need that personal connection.

It's crucial because without it you will find it difficult to get their perspective and explore how you can align rather than work against each other.

In his book *Supercommunicators: How to Unlock the Secret Language of Connection*, Pulitzer prize-winning reporter Charles Duhigg explains that we must do more than walk in someone else's shoes.[214] He believes that we need to go beyond imagining you are them, because of the inherent risk of incorrect assumptions (remember those?), and instead make a real effort to seek out the other person's perspective. We can get that perspective when we stop focusing on the facts and ask people how they feel.

This is sometimes harder than we think it will be. We tend to assume that people will find our questions intrusive, so instead of really digging in, we stick to inane small talk about the weather. In doing so, we miss out on opportunities to build rapport, show empathy and reciprocate by appropriately sharing our own vulnerability.

Duhigg shares multiple studies about how asking deeper questions and following up those questions with other deeper questions is often enough to make people start listening and question their assumptions.[215]

This holds true across industries and people. In another 2016 Harvard study, the researchers found that when people are asked questions, particularly

---

214 Duhigg, C. (2024). *Supercommunicators: How to Unlock the Secret Language of Connection.* Doubleday.
215 Duhigg. Supercommunicators.

follow-up questions, they are more likely to feel validated and heard and want to interact with that person in the future.[216] However, the follow-up questions must build on what the person shared and signal that their perspective is valued.[217]

Imagine you're controlling a sluice gate of insights that you can choose to open wider by asking respectful, probing questions. When the other person exposes their vulnerabilities, you match their vulnerability by expanding the opening of the sluice gates and revealing something about yourself. Then you keep asking questions – opening the gates wider and wider – but focusing on feelings, beliefs and motivations rather than facts. This is the way that you can gather the insights you need to develop your inter-relational expertise and centred leadership.

Remember to keep bringing the conversation back to the other person to avoid the trap of making the conversation all about you. This is an important reminder if you're like me and can sometimes get caught up in sharing a long-winded story.

Asking the right questions might sound daunting, but it's all about how you recast the questions. Duhigg says, 'If we ask questions that push people to think and talk about their values, beliefs and experiences and then reciprocate with emotions of our own, we can't help but listen to one another.'[218]

Instead of asking, 'What did you do over the weekend?', ask, 'What did you enjoy most about last weekend?'

216 Huang, K et al. (2017). 'It doesn't hurt to ask: Question-asking increases liking.' *Journal of Personality and Social Psychology.* https://www.hbs.edu/ris/Publication%20Files/ Huang%20et%20al%202017_6945bc5e-3b3e-4c0a-addd-254c9e603c60.pdf.
217 Huang. It doesn't hurt to ask.
218 Duhigg. Supercommunicators.

You'll immediately get beyond the weekend activity to an insight into what is important to the other person.

Instead of asking, 'How was your day?', try asking, 'What was the highlight of your day?' Again, this approach shifts the focus from a summary to an insight, and you'll learn a lot more about what makes the speaker tick.

As a centred leader you need to keep gathering those insights, and the next time stakeholder relations are challenging, you can draw on that pre-existing connection to explore the issue at hand. This will help you to avoid downplaying the person's thoughts and opinions because you'll know where they are coming from and how to keep exploring what's important to them.

On the other hand, when we simply agree to get along and don't bother to explore the deeper feelings of those we're in a dialogue with, we can miss opportunities. No one really loves conflict, but the right type of conflict can deepen a relationship and bring better, more innovative ideas and solutions to the surface. The upside is doing so can also deepen relationships and shared commitment to solutions and bring us all closer to centred leadership.

Shared interests build commitment to solutions

Inter-relational expertise warrants its own point in the Centring Star because complex change is often associated with complex interpersonal relationships. I strongly believe this because of my experiences leading complex employee negotiations when a system was in turmoil.

It was early 2005, and over the preceding 18 months, I had been working to understand the specific problems driving public-sector doctors out of the system and exploring potential options in readiness for enterprise bargaining negotiations, which were expected to be tense. During the bargaining preparation phase, I worked closely with the equivalent of the Deputy Chief Executive, who was responsible for every publicly-run health service in the State.

As the State Government prepared to negotiate pay and conditions with public sector doctors, the Dr Jayant Patel scandal, often called 'Queensland's Dr Death' case, began to surface.[219]

Patel had worked as a surgeon at Bundaberg Base Hospital in Queensland. A nurse working with him started raising concerns about his practices as early as 2003. But it wasn't until two years later that it all came to a head. This was during the Queensland Estimates Committee process, a mechanism the Queensland Parliament uses to scrutinise how government departments and agencies spend public money.

The Estimates Committee is supposed to allow members of parliament to ask government ministers and senior officials detailed questions about their

---

219 (25 May 2005). 'Queensland's "Dr Death" linked to 80 deaths.' *The Age.* https://www.theage.com.au/national/queenslands-dr-death-linked-to-80-deaths-20050525-ge089n.html.

spending plans and how public money is being used to ensure transparency and accountability. However, often politicians cherry-pick questions likely to embarrass or discredit their political opponents, even if those questions don't directly relate to the budget or the main focus of dialogue. And this was the case with the Estimates Committee hearings that year.

The opposition asked the executive I had been preparing for the negotiations specific, pointed questions about what the health department knew about Dr Patel's practices and how it responded. They wanted to show that, as the Health Minister, Gordon Nuttall had either ignored or failed to act on warnings about Dr Patel.

The short story is that a public official or executive participating in an Estimates Committee hearing can potentially be held criminally liable if they mislead Parliament. The truth came out, and the Health Minister was subsequently jailed after being charged with perjury and corruption in relation to other matters.

The full scope of Dr Patel's misconduct, including multiple patient deaths and surgical complications, came to public attention during subsequent formal inquiries in 2005, a Commission of Inquiry and a Health Systems Review.

Although the inquiry focused on systemic issues and did not blame either the Chief Executive or his Deputy, both were removed from their positions. It was not a great time to begin bargaining with public-sector doctors, who had been deserting the public system in droves due to pay and conditions and now felt their reputations were under attack as well.

To make matters more challenging, the government decided to let the doctors have a separate enterprise bargaining agreement. This meant that more than half of the doctors who voted had to support any agreement reached, whereas previously, any doctor who voted against reaching an agreement could be overwhelmed by the voting preferences of the vast number of other workers in the health system.

We needed to do something to get the outcomes we needed for our doctors and our health care system. But bunkering down in position-based bargaining would have led to significant industrial action, which would have hurt the people needing health care. So, we took a different approach.

Somehow, I ended up as Queensland Health's lead negotiator. Michael Klug, a barrister well-known for his work as a mediator and a pioneer in alternative dispute resolution in Australia, was engaged to help us try something different, less damaging to the community and hopefully better for everyone.

To do this the negotiating teams were expanded beyond the typical government and union officials to include doctors who worked as health administrators on the management team and senior and junior doctors delivering health care on the union team. And because of these new perspectives, we were able to find outcomes that addressed most of the key system-level barriers to attraction and retention of the various categories of doctors. It was an extremely complex situation where negotiations occurred in parallel with the inquiry, review, extensive media commentary and rear-guard action from senior doctors who refused to follow the union.

What we did significantly influenced my approach to leading complex change in all aspects of leadership over many years. I experienced first-hand the value of cooperation, understanding each other's needs and finding solutions that benefit both sides rather than just winning at the other party's expense.

Interest-based bargaining

During my time as Queensland Health's lead negotiator, we adopted an interest-based bargaining (IBB) approach. IBB is also called 'win-win' bargaining or 'principled negotiation' and is a strategy in which both sides collaborate to address each party's underlying interests rather than just their stated positions.

By following four key principles, we were able to focus on the issues and deepen our understanding of the problem during a period of significant conflict, where a splinter group of doctors started meeting at the Pineapple Hotel (known as the Pineapple Group) and making their demands outside of formal channels. The four key principles we focused on were:

1. **Focus on interests, not positions:** In interest-based bargaining, instead of sticking to rigid positions (e.g., 'I want a 10% pay raise'), both parties explore the reasons behind these positions (e.g., 'I need a raise because I don't feel valued as a clinician'). The words used were something like, 'We're treated like @#$%! so you can pay us more for putting up with it'. This shifts the conversation to finding ways to meet both parties' real needs.

2. **Take a collaborative approach:** The process encourages working together, not against each other. Both sides share their concerns openly and brainstorm solutions that address everyone's interests, avoiding a win-lose scenario.

3. **Problem-solve together:** Rather than treating the negotiation as a battle, interest-based bargaining views it as a problem both sides are trying to solve. For example, if a company can't afford a 10% raise, the employees and employer might find other ways to provide value, like benefits that mean more to the employees than they cost the employer or increased flexibility in work arrangements.

4. **Look for mutual gains:** The goal is to reach an agreement where both sides feel they've gained. This builds stronger relationships and often leads to more sustainable agreements.

I knew we were on to something from the first session Michael Klug facilitated. The management and union teams were sent to different rooms and asked to develop a list of their top 10 interests, i.e., the core needs, goals and values that matter most to them in the negotiation process.

When we reconvened and shared our lists, we discovered that only one interest differed. It was no surprise that the union team wanted to maximise the doctor's income, and the management team wanted to minimise the state's costs.

The dynamic shifted when everyone realised we had nine other interests in common, including community access to care, patient safety and treating staff well. We used the lens of those shared interests to jointly explore the challenges facing the system and the doctors working in it.

It wasn't an easy road, but we weren't at war. We were working towards finding solutions that met our shared interests and gave each of us some wins in those areas where we differed. Over the following months, we holed up, three days a week, in a conference room overlooking the Brisbane River. We explored the problems and assessed the suitability of many potential solutions.

Unfortunately, we reached a point where people not involved in the process had a role to play, like approving the funding that could be used to pay for the solutions. Those people also tried to dictate the formal offer that could be presented to the unions.

Thankfully, after some highly persuasive conversations, sense prevailed.

On the day we presented the government offer, I was authorised to walk into the room and announce we had more than $700 million to work with. The powers above had agreed that instead of presenting a formal offer, we could continue to work together and design a package of terms and conditions that met the interests of all parties within that funding envelope.

We achieved that goal. We worked together to educate doctors about the package, all while the Pineapple Group collectively heckled members of the management and union teams in staff information sessions. Despite an aggressive anti-agreement campaign by the Pineapple Group, a majority of doctors voted in support of the proposed agreement.

It was certified, but the Pineapple Group kept going. They targeted politicians navigating a challenging public relations situation until further concessions were made, and the State's doctors received a package of benefits worth approximately $1 billion.

This didn't just play out in my professional life. As lead negotiator for the government department, I had to manage internal and external stakeholder relationships, but I also had a husband, two small children, and other family and friends with whom I had relationships. I also had a relationship with myself.

Much of this book has delved into who you are as a leader, your self-awareness, and the choices you can make about how you want others to experience you as a leader and human being because your relationship with yourself and others is critical.

When you lead complex change, conflict is inevitable. How you choose to relate to other people and engage with conflict will either position you for success or make your life a misery. This is why your inter-relational expertise is so crucial. Remember to tether yourself to your Centring Star – use your values and character strengths and focus on the points of the star that will enable you to navigate the external world – the points we're exploring in the last chapter, this one and the next. They are like the points on a compass and will enable you to find your way between the eyes of the storms you will inevitably encounter.

CHAPTER 9

Centring with Tactical Agility

In the previous two chapters we explored two outer points of the Centring Star, focusing on contextual wisdom and inter-relational expertise. Now we turn to the final point – tactical agility – and how this can be used to navigate the unpredictability of complex change, and stay the course as centred leaders, adapting to what emerges with flexibility and adaptability. Tactical agility as a centring point helps you to sense and respond to the evolving landscape around you.

Understanding and embracing tactical agility

Three years after the pandemic began, COVID-19 finally caught up with me. I wasn't a close contact, and I have no idea where I contracted the virus or why it took so long when it had been in our house before.

It made me think about how, in the late 1800s, scientists Louis Pasteur and Robert Koch discovered that microscopic germs, including bacteria, spread infections and caused illness.[220] This was a ground-breaking discovery, but why some people get sick while others don't has continued to intrigue scientists for centuries.

The limits of cause and effect

Searching for a specific cause when faced with complex problems is like looking for a needle in a haystack. The effort you put into finding someone or something to blame is unlikely to yield any useful results and distracts you from how you will respond.

One danger of tackling complex problems is that we can be lured into seeking linear cause-and-effect explanations. This is a mistake because complex problems often have multiple causes and are difficult to predict.[221] The causal ambiguity makes it difficult to determine causality when multiple factors are present and interact in complex ways.[222]

Developing your adaptative capacity is the way forward

Instead of pinpointing blame, it's better to accept what cannot be changed and focus on developing your adaptive capacity and capability to respond to complex challenges. This is the way that you can continue to reassess where you are, and continually move from the midst of the storms, back into

---

220 (2004). *National Research Council (US) Committee to Update Science, Medicine, and Animals. Science, Medicine, and Animals.* National Academies Press.

221 Morieux, Y & Tollman, P. (2014). *Six Simple Rules: How to Manage Complexity without Getting Complicated.* Harvard Business Review Press.

222 Morieux. Six Simple Rules.

the calm that's the eye of the storm. When you embrace adaptation, you're better able to make sense of what is happening or could happen now or in the future and better able to focus your energies on responding appropriately. By embracing a mindset of continuous learning and adaptation, you can better equip yourself to face the challenges of today's rapidly-changing business landscape.

Flexible, agile, and adaptive approaches work during times of complex change. Satya Nadella took over as CEO of Microsoft in 2014 at a time of significant uncertainty and change in the technology industry.[223] He recognised the need to adapt to changing consumer preferences and emerging technologies and to move away from the company's traditional focus on software and hardware.[224]

Under Nadella's leadership, Microsoft has embraced a more flexible and agile approach to product development, with a greater emphasis on cloud-based services and mobile devices. Nadella has also strongly emphasised empathy and inclusivity, recognising the importance of diverse perspectives in driving innovation. His flexible and visionary approach has allowed Microsoft to stay ahead of the curve in a rapidly evolving industry and positioned Microsoft as a leader in cloud computing and digital services.

He reminds us, 'If you take two people, one of them is a learn-it-all and the other one is a know-it-all, the learn-it-all will always trump the know-it-all in the long run, even if they start with less innate capability.'[225]

The next time something goes wrong on your path to achieving complex change, resist the urge to find out why at all costs. First, consider whether

------

223 Nadella, S. (2017). *Hit Refresh: The Quest to Rediscover Microsoft's Soul and Imagine a Better Future for Everyone.* HarperCollins.

224 Nadella. Hit Refresh.

225 Bass, D. (4 August 2016). 'Satya Nadella Talks Microsoft at Middle Aged.' Bloomberg. https://www.bloomberg.com/features/2016-satya-nadella-interview-issue/.

what you discover will be worth investing time and effort. Then, decide if you're better off putting that time and effort into building your capacity to adapt, learn and respond. I've always believed in working towards what's next and most helpful, rather than getting bogged down in trying to understand what was. This is tactical agility.

What is tactical agility and why does it matter?

Tactical agility focuses on helping people do the right work at the right time to deliver more value. Tactical agility requires agility in both thought and action. Before jumping in with what you believe is the solution to a problem, you should seek out data and information from diverse sources and stand back to see the bigger picture. Even better, if you have time, draw a rich picture.

However, avoid analysis paralysis. I often think of finding my way through complex change environments as like surfing a wave – not that I can surf! However, when surfing you need to sense and respond to how the currents form the waves you must ride.

Philosopher Alan Watts, known for emphasising the importance of flexible thinking, adaptation to change and a holistic approach to problem-solving, is often quoted as having said, 'The only way to make sense out of change is to plunge into it, move with it, and join the dance.'

His works are extensive, and it has been challenging to confirm the source of the quote. However, I'm sharing it because it so clearly sums up the meaning of tactical agility.

You can't learn anything or progress change unless you join the fray! However, when you do, it's all about how you show up, make sense of your context, respond, learn, review and then do it all again. Sometimes, the music track you're dancing to will change. You may or may not see it coming but you always adjust your dancing style to suit the rhythm of the music. That is tactical agility, and you will need this to lead through uncertain, complex times.

Avoid waiting and watching in uncertain times

How often have you felt frustrated with the accuracy of your local weather forecast? You have plans to go camping or host an outdoor event, so you diligently check the forecast and confirm it's expected to be fine. But then it rains buckets, spoiling your plans. Or you cancel your plans because of a predicted severe storm that never eventuates.

We accept that we cannot control the weather. However, this is only one of the many other systems that interact with each other and influence our lives, work and the change we'd like to see.

For example, the Reserve Bank raises interest rates, which reduces consumer spending. Natural disasters push up the prices of fresh produce and insurance premiums, and governments must be careful that attempts to reduce cost-of-living pressures don't have adverse consequences. Meanwhile, corporations are re-adjusting their sails post-pandemic to trim what's no longer needed or trying to recoup losses.

Just like the Bureau of Meteorology tries to predict the weather, consumers, businesses and governments cannot say with certainty what will happen with the economy. It's also difficult to predict how our roles and work will be impacted, but that doesn't mean we should do nothing. And although our instincts are hard-wired to fear the unknown, we should tap into the potential opportunities that the unknown presents.

In his book, *The Antidote: Happiness for People Who Can't Stand Positive Thinking*, Oliver Burkeman says, 'Uncertainty is where things happen. It is where the opportunities – for success, for happiness, for really living –are waiting.'[226]

He suggests we learn from Stoicism, an ancient philosophy.[227] A Stoic would tell us to focus on what is within our control and let go of attachment to what is beyond our influence.

However, Stoic wisdom also reminds us that uncertainty holds inherent opportunities for growth and learning. By accepting your operating environment's inherent unpredictability, you can become more open to exploring new avenues, innovating and embracing calculated risks.

Because macro changes such as technology disruption, regulatory change, market dynamics and global events are outside your control, you may be tempted to adopt a wait-and-see approach. That's a mistake if you want to be a centred leader because familiarity with volatile contexts and habitually adopting a passive stance could see you lose strategic advantages and inadvertently increase your team's stress level.

When I debrief people on their Indicator of Ambiguity profile, I consistently see them underestimate the impact their ease with ambiguity is having on their teams, especially if they also have a strong sense of how they want to be perceived by others. Not only are most humans wired so that ambiguity and uncertainty are stress-inducing, we are also wired to make sense of what we see, and to experience things based on what we already know.

---

226 Burkeman, O. (2013). *The Antidote: Happiness for People Who Can't Stand Positive Thinking*. Farrar, Straus and Giroux.
227 Burkeman. The Antidote.

Your team could see the situation in vastly different ways from you. Some will see potential strategic advantages, and others will see the beginning of the end of the world.

If you want to amplify the people who see potential strategic advantages:

1. Avoid the desire for others to perceive you're on top of everything.

2. Learn from but don't be constrained by the past.

3. Invite your team to embrace the unknown and collectively engage with new ideas, different perspectives, and different people whilst exploring complex challenges one step at a time.

Tackling uncertainty alone is like assembling a jigsaw puzzle in the dark. Involving others turns on the lights, allowing different pieces to come together more clearly and quickly through shared insights and experiences. It generates more agile strategies and lays out new paths through the storms you'll face as a leader.

Why AQ matters as much as EQ and IQ

Many years ago, I worked with a woman who was proud of her Mensa membership. Though she had reasonable EQ (emotional quotient or your ability to sense emotion in yourself and in others), the evolving work environment proved challenging. Her career stalled, and after several restructures, she no longer fit in. Despite her confidence and resistance to retirement, she struggled with rapid changes and constant disruptions.

Her reliance on past successes and high IQ status made her resistant to new approaches. Eventually, our manager assigned her basic support roles below her pay grade due to a lack of trust in her adaptability.

AQ – or your adaptability quotient – is the ability to adjust to change, learn from experience and overcome adversity. It measures how well you cope with uncertainty, complexity and ambiguity. It's a very different beast from EQ, which is the ability to use your emotions as a source of information and motivation. EQ helps you empathise, collaborate and communicate with others, but AQ takes it a step further. It helps you innovate, experiment and create with others. EQ helps you fit in, but AQ helps you stand out. EQ helps you bring people with you, but AQ helps you lead them to the other side of a complex change.

One of the benefits of AQ is that it allows you to see intelligence not as a static quality you possess or lack but as a dynamic process that depends on the interaction between you, the task and the situation. This means you can enhance your adaptive intelligence by selecting tasks and situations that build on your strengths and adapting your approach to tasks and situations that challenge you.

Being very emotionally intelligent also has its downsides because, although people with high EQ can be creative, they are more commonly great at collaboration and conformity rather than challenging the status quo and introducing new ideas. They avoid ruffling feathers.[228]

My colleague could have thought of herself as a jazz musician rather than a Mensa member—a jazz musician who does not rely on a fixed score but rather improvises with skill and flair, who does not play alone but rather collaborates with other musicians and who does not repeat the same tunes but

---

228 Chamorro-Prumizic, T & Yearsley, A. (13 January 2017). 'The Downsides of Being Very Emotionally Intelligent.' *Harvard Business Review.* https://hbr.org/2017/01/the-downsides-of-being-very-emotionally-intelligent.

rather creates new variations and combinations. This would have supported her to explore new ways of responding to increase her AQ.

Pulitzer Prize-winning author Ray Bradbury summed up AQ when he said, 'You've got to jump off cliffs all the time and build your wings on the way down.'[229] This is good advice when you're stepping out from the calm of the eye into the storm as well.

Stack the skills you use

Since becoming an accredited partner with AdaptiQMinds and engaging with the research and evidence about tolerance of ambiguity and complexity, I've been experimenting with the eight skills that enable people to embrace the unknown.[230]

The interesting thing is the skills are not specific to building tolerance of ambiguity. When cultivated as habits they provide a wonderful toolkit for adapting to emerging complexity and achieving changes.

Evidence shows us eight skills that are positively correlated with building tolerance of ambiguity. They're also valuable skills for adapting to emerging complexity too. They can be stacked in different combinations to help you develop your AQ and respond to the unknown while navigating complex change. I like to think of them as a group of skills superpowers.

---

229 Associated Press. (27 November 1990). 'Bradbury's advice: "jump".' *Trenton Evening Times.* (GenealogyBank).

230 O'Connor, P et al. (2022). 'Leader tolerance of ambiguity: Implications for follower performance outcomes in high and low ambiguous work situations.' *The Journal of Applied Behavioral Science*; O'Connor, P, Becker, K & Fewster, K. (2018). 'Tolerance of ambiguity at work predicts leadership, job performance, and creativity.' In Creating Uncertainty Conference. https://eprints.qut.edu.au/120614/1/Tolerance%20of%20Ambiguity_2018. pdf.

Each time you feel that instinctual fight, flight or freeze response, choose which of the skills superpowers will be most useful in your current context. Then keep working your way through them in different combinations to either find your way to the centre of the storm or work out the next right thing to do as you head out into the storm again.

My recommendation is to avoid following a strict order in their use and always tailor the combination you use to the context and how it evolves. So what are these skills superpowers?

Skills Superpowers

1. **Mindfulness:** paying full attention to what's happening right now.

    It's about noticing your thoughts, feelings, and surroundings without judging them. Ambiguity during complex change can lead to stress because it's full of unknowns. Mindfulness keeps you focused on what's happening now and helps you to think more clearly. When you're not stressed about what could happen, you make better choices with the information you have.

2. **Creativity:** connecting seemingly unrelated ideas, using what already exists in different ways including adding, subtracting, or combining elements to forge new solutions and approaches.

    It's essential for enabling innovation and problem-solving. It often emerges from making connections in the subconscious. It's about recognising patterns and possibilities that are not immediately obvious, which can be particularly valuable in ambiguous situations.

3. **Flexible thinking:** adapting and changing methods as new situations arise.

It's about exploring different perspectives and information to make more sense of a situation. It's about taking calculated risks rather than jumping into solutions and understanding the larger context first. This helps identify the main issues and guide more effective strategies. It prevents you from getting lost in the details before the overall goals are clear and stops you from sticking to one solution that may not work as things evolve.

4. **Unlocking inertia:** when you get stuck, it's like being caught in quicksand. The more you struggle the deeper you sink.

   Break free from that paralysing hold by taking small, deliberate steps forward. Identify a starting point and focus on manageable actions to overcome that sense of being stuck.

5. **Finding focus:** to cut through the fog of uncertainty.

   Carve out space and time to concentrate on what you know and can control rather than getting overwhelmed by what you don't know. This clarity better equips you to identify and act on the most relevant factors and options.

6. **Curiosity:** the desire to learn more about something.

   Curiosity helps you see situations as chances to learn something new instead of just feeling stressed. When navigating complex change, curiosity means you want to understand new ideas or discover why things happen. Being curious makes you ask more questions and consider different viewpoints.

7. **Assertiveness:** brings clarity.

   Assertiveness helps you clarify the unknown by asking direct questions and setting clear expectations. Invite your team to share their ideas and perspectives early. This diversity of thought can lead to better, more creative solutions.

8. **Courageous action:** means stepping beyond what's comfortable despite feeling unsure.

   Consider 'what if' ideas. These can prevent immediate reactions like fight, flight or freeze, and enable logical thinking and constructive actions by focusing on being more emotionally agile.

Influence at the edges

When you're trying to integrate all five points of the star to become a centred leader, and lead your team through times of complex change, it's tempting to want to change everything at once, but it's often more effective to influence the system gradually. Nudges and subtle interventions that alter the decision environment can help individuals make better decisions.

In the early 2000s, hospitals struggled with hospital-acquired infections. Traditional education campaigns and training programs failed to significantly improve hand hygiene compliance among healthcare workers. Then, studies found that nudging – using techniques like visible reminders, strategic placement of nudges and seeking individual feedback – significantly increased compliance from 48% to 66%.[231]

Over time, these interventions, such as strategically placing hand sanitiser dispensers at hospital room entrances, were widely adopted and evolved through further experimentation to create a real difference in hand hygiene compliance.

---

231 Pittet, D. (2000). Improving compliance with hand hygiene in hospitals. Infection Control & Hospital Epidemiology. https://pubmed.ncbi.nlm.nih.gov/10879568/.

In the same way, your own nudges and subtle interventions could make a big difference to the changes you want to see. They may light a small spark that eventually grows into a bushfire under the right conditions. If you're struggling to gain traction for your change, focus on smaller, manageable changes that can later be leveraged.

Small, targeted changes help test your system responses as well. Trying small changes helps you quickly learn what works. When you see positive reactions, nudge things further in the desired direction with incremental moves that don't overwhelm the system.

If you're starting to feel frustrated, remember that small, continuous improvements are better than no change and are often safer. Amplify successful strategies and stop wasting time on lost causes by creating feedback loops that provide early insights and inform ongoing decisions.

However, given that your Centring Star is tethered to your values and character strengths it's imperative that you keep your nudges aligned. Harvard professor Cass Sunstein said in an interview with McKinsey about the evolution of nudging: 'Good nudges still make the chooser's life better, and bad nudges don't.'[232]

Treat complex change like a treasure hunt

When you have tactical agility, then you're in a much better position to treat complex change like a treasure hunt. In my first senior executive role, I was expected to enable triple the number of medical graduates to complete their

---

232 Fusaro, R & Sperling-Magro, J. (6 August 2021). 'Much anew about "nudging". McKinsey. https://www.mckinsey.com/capabilities/strategy-and-corporate-finance/our-insights/much-anew-about-nudging.

mandatory training before capacity would be significantly exceeded within three years. I could have felt extremely anxious with this task. In fact, many people believed this increase was akin to responding to a tsunami.

However, rather than feeling overwhelmed, I was excited. These future doctors would care for me and my family, so maintaining training standards was paramount. I knew the complexity of the challenge meant I wouldn't be solving it alone. Numerous smart people in the system could help surface options and solutions.

Rather than being overwhelmed by the complexity, I saw it as a treasure hunt (where I would need to use my tactical agility). A hunt where hidden gems of knowledge, insights and opportunities were waiting to be discovered.

We started with an options paper that included safe solutions that we knew wouldn't go far enough as well as 'out there' ideas that challenged people's thinking. We met with many people, including the frontline doctors training new graduates completing their medical internship.

In the first year, we didn't make much progress. However, when we asked people to respond to an options paper the next year, some of our ideas started to bear fruit. People began to adopt some of our original 'out there' solutions as their own, and some frontline doctors proposed even more innovative solutions.

Our role shifted from generating ideas to stewarding the best ones through the bureaucracy of government and accreditation bodies. We kept asking, 'What's stopping this from happening?' and 'Can we change it?'

Though doubts crept in, as psychologist Susan Jeffers said, I chose to 'feel the fear and do it anyway'.[233] By working together collectively, we ultimately succeeded.

The next time a complex challenge arises, ask yourself, 'Is this for me to solve alone, or to lead the process?' Knowing you're not alone makes navigating complex change less stressful and more fun.

Creativity enables you to shift gears

Tactical agility requires creativity, and the reason that it matters is because creative thinking is what enables you to shift gears. However, many people confuse creativity with artistry.

Everyone in my immediate family can at least draw an elephant's backside. Some of them can do far more than that, including my daughter who is studying design. But not me.

That doesn't mean I am not creative. I made my wedding dress, all the bridesmaids' dresses, the flower girl's dress, and the groom's vest to match my dress. I even made boxer shorts for the men in the bridal party who then performed in them to a certain Right Said Fred song at the reception. Everything looked fine, except for my brother's boxer shorts – they ended up more like a G-string, which he chose not to wear.

In my much younger years, I was in a theatre company. Over the years, I made costumes and clothes for the kids, dabbled in card-making, mosaics and garden design, spent hours making elaborate kids' birthday cakes, and even made a paper mâché horse pinata that my then five-year-old son could sit on and pretend to ride.

---

233 Jeffers, S. (2017). *Feel the Fear and Do it Anyway.* Vermilion.

However, I assumed I was not creative because I'm not good at drawing, and my painting skills tend towards the highly abstract. I made the mistake of comparing my lack of artistry to the rest of my family. But in fact, I was very creative in other ways.

Creativity is an often-underrated and under-recognised part of tactical agility, and therefore centred leadership. In fact, creative thinking was identified as one of the single most important skills we can have - ranked just below analytical thinking in the World Economic Forum's *Future Jobs Report 2023*.[234] Employers ranked it ahead of resilience, flexibility and agility because workers must be creative to adapt to disrupted workplaces.[235]

The World Economic Forum also found creative thinking is 'increasing in importance relative to analytical thinking as workplace tasks become increasingly automated'.[236]

With the anticipated pace and nature of change at work, we must remember that creative thinking is a treasure hunt without a map, while analytical thinking is assembling IKEA furniture with the manual. Unfortunately, being given the right manual for every change is highly unlikely. So we must tap into our creativity to find solutions to the challenges that will inevitably emerge.

Studies have shown that creativity has significant linkages with all but one of the superpowers that build tolerance of ambiguity – for good reason.[237] Creativity requires us to let our minds wander and ruminate on different aspects of a problem, which risks us getting stuck in inertia – that's why unlocking inertia is another of the skills superpowers. We need to use our tactical agility to find creative ways to understand and respond to the context

---

234 (30 April 2023). 'The Future of Jobs Report 2023.' [Report.] World Economic Forum.
      https://www.weforum.org/publications/the-future-of-jobs-report-2023/.
235 The Future of Jobs Report 2023.
236 The Future of Jobs Report 2023.
237 O'Connor. Leader tolerance of ambiguity; O'Connor. Tolerance of ambiguity at work.

and manage relationships with inter-relational expertise. Creativity is a superpower because it unlocks new possibilities by leveraging what already exists.

That requires sitting and playing with your thoughts but the secret is to ruminate without getting stuck. One solution is to set a timer or use other constraints that push you out of thought and into action.

Four minutes is all you need according to Hal Gregerson, MIT Leadership Centre's Executive Director.[238] He recommends using those four minutes for a 'question burst' process of rapidly brainstorming questions, not answers, to challenge existing assumptions. His research has found that question bursts unlock new perspectives and innovative solutions quickly.[239]

So, next time you're looking for an answer, try digging deeper with a rapid round of questions first. This can help you tap into your own creativity and build out your tactical agility.

Play with change models

Another way that you can embrace tactical agility is through playing with different change models. Imagine that you're leading a major change initiative in your organisation (this may not be too far from reality!). You have a clear vision of what you want to achieve, a detailed plan of action and a strong team of supporters. You are confident that you can follow the plan and deliver the expected results. Sounds good, right?

I must ask, what decade do you think you're in?

---

238 Gregersen, H. (2018). *Questions are the answer: A breakthrough approach to your most vexing problems at work and in life.* HarperCollins.

239 Gregersen. Questions are the answer.

Change management used to be all about setting a clear goal upfront and pushing all efforts in that direction. But nowadays, it's not uncommon for everything to change partway through implementing a plan. This might be because the external environment becomes more volatile and unpredictable or is never stable, internal stakeholders have different opinions and expectations and industry approaches are shifting rapidly in response to broader system impacts. You realise that your original plan is no longer relevant or feasible and that you have no idea what the outcome will look like. How do you feel? Confused, frustrated, anxious, overwhelmed?

One of my coaching clients has been experiencing this. They are amid a major change process, but it's uncertain where that change will land. They feel like they're in a forest, unable to see the trees and with a heavy sense of uncertainty about what the future will look like for that part of their organisation. Where it will land could be anyone's guess.

This is not uncommon, and it's why we need to talk about the importance of helping people with change in the best way possible rather than rigidly clinging to any one change model or framework.

Managing the volatility of change can feel like you're riding a roller coaster blindfolded. You anticipate ups and downs and unexpected twists, but you don't see the end until you arrive. Tactical agility is an approach to achieving change that is all about adapting and learning as you go rather than sticking to a fixed and very detailed plan. It's also how you keep yourself and your team centred and focused on your strategic goal despite the volatility and uncertainty you'll be experiencing.

It can be even more challenging if you are working with consultants on a project that influences system change. If you and they adopt a traditional consulting approach, you're setting yourself up for failure.

If multiple studies suggest an estimated 70% of organisational change initiatives fail[240], and systemic reviews question the evidence behind many change models, why would you let one model constrain your efforts?

A more flexible approach lets you adjust plans as you learn new things and situations change. It's like updating your route on a GPS based on live traffic updates.

Valuable upsides to this more flexible approach to change include:

- Trying new ideas and learning from them to allow more creative solutions to emerge that might have been otherwise missed.

- Developing organisational resilience while everyone is changing and getting better at handling uncertainties and adjusting to changes as they happen.

However, without a clear end goal, team members might feel unsure about their roles and future, which can lower morale if not managed well. Using resources efficiently can also be harder when goals are not fixed. You risk burning people out if you use too much effort or change plans too often.

If you're finding yourself amongst hurly-burly change, you may want to:

- **Focus on managing uncertainty.** Ensure you have a strong focus on managing uncertainty and the lack of clarity for yourself and others. Notice your personal responses and impact on others and be curious about other people's experiences.

  Consider using credible tools and frameworks like the SCARF Model developed by Dr. David Rock of the NeuroLeadership Institute, to understand and enable management of workplace

---

240 Nohria, N & Beer, M. (2000). 'Cracking the Code of Change.' *Harvard Business Review.* https://hbr.org/2000/05/cracking-the-code-of-change.

social interactions using five key domains: Status, Certainty, Autonomy, Relatedness, and Fairness.[241] This model is especially relevant in managing uncertainty because it provides a structured way to identify and mitigate potential stressors.

- **Keep everyone informed.** To reduce uncertainty and build trust, start communicating early, be transparent, use multiple channels, repeat key messages, make it easy for people to provide feedback and tailor your messages for different audiences to help them embrace the change.

- **Empower people.** Empower your people by giving them the skills and authority to make decisions. Ensure people are familiar with the eight skills superpowers for tolerating ambiguity, improving performance and well-being. Then, work with your team to develop a shared understanding of core principles for delegated decision-making to reduce the cognitive load and result in quicker and more confident decision-making.

- **Use skills superpowers.** Use those skills superpowers when you block out regular time to explore what's working, what isn't, what's changed, what goals need to be adjusted and what decisions need to be made.

- **Avoid rigid adherence to a single change model.** Avoid desperately clinging to one change management model at all costs. Hold different models lightly and play with what works best for the specific context.

---

241 'Welcome to the SCARF Assessment.' [Assessment tool]. NeuroLeadership Institute. https://neuroleadership.com/research/tools/nli-scarf-assessment/; (17 October 2023). '5 Ways to Spark (or Destroy) Your Employees' Motivation.' NeuroLeadership Institute. https://neuroleadership.com/your-brain-at-work/scarf-model-motivate-your-employees.

As Jeff Bezos, the founder of Amazon says, 'We humans coevolve with our tools. We change our tools, and then our tools change us.'[242]

Embracing your own Centring Star?

Tactical agility is not just about reacting quickly. It's also about thoughtfully adapting to change, thriving through ambiguity and embracing uncertainty while turning these into opportunities for growth. This point of the star equips you with the mindset and tools to navigate complex situations with grace and purpose, leading your teams through the chaos of the storms and from the relative calm of one eye of the storm to the next.

As we move forward, taking action steps to align with our own Centring Star, remember that the outer engagement points of the star are all interconnected. Contextual wisdom informs your understanding of the environment, inter-relational expertise strengthens your focus on and interactions with others and tactical agility empowers you to make the most of each challenge that you will inevitably face. By integrating these elements, along with all the thinking and feeling elements of your inner engagement points of the Centring Star, you create a dynamic leadership approach, one that can guide you through the storms of a VUCA and BANI world, and help you remain centred no matter how many storms converge.

---

242 Bezos, J & Isaacson, W. (2020). *Invent and Wander: The Collected Writings of Jeff Bezos.* Harvard Business Review Press.

CONCLUSION

This book has taken you on a journey through the challenges likely to face leaders who want to make a difference and effect real change. Our focus has been on how you can find your centre despite – or perhaps hand-in-hand with – the chaos. And then continually re-find it if (and when) you're knocked off course and back into the storms again.

As we've found, becoming a centred leader isn't a one-way journey that begins at point A and ends once you've achieved point B. Instead, it's a continuous cycle of learning, application and adaptation, that leads you to constantly seek out and move between the calm spaces at the centre of the storms. So, in the same way, this book isn't designed to deliver everything that you need to implement these actions, but to spark your own personal reflection, conversation and action.

Most importantly, this journey is about understanding that you are not your context. You are not – and do not have to be – defined by the storms you find yourself in. When the storms do start to rage, it's easy to fall into the trap of being shaped by the chaos swirling around you. Many leaders, including myself, have succumbed to the busyness, been overwhelmed and lost their centre for a while. But, as we've found, you have a choice.

As you sail your ship towards the complex change you are seeking to achieve, you may wish to think of yourself as a captain steering through uncharted waters. You must rely on your compass – your values, beliefs, and character strengths – to guide your decisions and actions in an environment where the weather is uncertain. Storms could emerge and converge at any time, but your acceptance of what is, and your ability to adapt and seek input from a diverse range of experts, will enable you to chart a course through the complex challenges and balance between the different currents and weather conditions.

This book is a guide for you, your team and your organisation. It offers a pathway that can help you pull back, reset and find your own centre to foster a stronger more dynamic leadership style based on the guidance of the Centring Star framework. From self-awareness and reflection to contextual wisdom and tactical agility, we've explored the elements that form the foundation of centred leadership, and which will give you what you need to navigate through the storms of a VUCA world.

The aim isn't just to withstand the storm, but to use it as an opportunity to grow, innovate and lead with clarity and purpose. The progress you make each day depends on your own conscious choices and the actions you take based on those choices.

As you align with your values and character strengths and use your Centring Star to navigate, you'll find yourself better equipped to respond to uncertainty and complexity every day. You'll also be better able to empower your team and those they support to do the same, creating a ripple effect that enhances your team, your organisation and even your industry.

Instead of seeing change as a negative experience your leadership will enable them to experience changing more positively and unlock both impact and growth – for people and business.

The key to staying the course of this journey is to not be overwhelmed by the process. Start small – and take one step at a time. Whether that means initiating a single conversation, experimenting with a new approach or practising creativity in a time of ambiguity, each action can build on the next. Leading by example, you'll inspire others to embrace change and become part of your journey towards centred leadership.

I'd love to hear about your experiences as you put these concepts into practice. My hope is that the ideas you've learned about in this book will help you navigate the storms you encounter and support you to embark on your own centred leadership journey!

WORK WITH SUSANNE

Susanne has a rare ability to switch between taking an analytical view and nurturing emotional connections. Her ability to see the big picture and her experience navigating rapidly changing contexts and collaborating with stakeholders puts her in an excellent position to help clients navigate complex change and adapt in the face of adversity.

Her approach is informed by academic research, validated tools and real-world experience, and is designed to put you in a position to respond well to complex problems, engage meaningfully with stakeholders, facilitate better teamwork and successfully handle change – for yourself and others.

Susanne's ability to be both warm and objective is an advantage when the situation demands emotional complexity. Her unique mix of perceptive insights, sensitivity, intuition, creative experimentation and coaching approach will help you build the skills and confidence you need to adapt and thrive in complex environments. Working with Susanne you'll experience noticeably positive results in your personal life as well as your career because you'll be so much less stressed and affected by pressure and indecision.

Susanne believes that everyone can change and that even the most complex world can be navigated. Sometimes you do have to figure out how to reconnect with yourself first, but once you start doing that deeper work, things will really start falling into place.

How to work with Susanne

- Keynote Speaking
- Centred Leadership Development Programs
- Gamified Training and Team Building Experiences featuring Ambiguity Apocalypse®
- Stakeholder Facilitation and Engagement
- Executive Coaching and Mentoring
- Consulting

Get in touch

Book a time to chat with Susanne here:
www.susanneleboutillier.com/contact/
or contact Susanne at **susanne@lebout.com.au** or +61 412 181 635.

Take a look at Susanne's website at **www.susanneleboutillier.com** to find out more about working with her.

Scan below to sign up for Susanne's email newsletter. You can unsubscribe at any time.

Printed in the USA
CPSIA information can be obtained
at www.ICGtesting.com
CBHW030926201124
17650CB00029B/1048